BEGINNING WORKBOOK

THE OXFORD
Picture
Dictionary

MARJORIE FUCHS

Oxford University Press

Oxford University Press
198 Madison Avenue, New York, NY 10016 USA
Great Clarendon Street, Oxford OX2 6DP England

Oxford New York

Auckland Cape Town Dar es Salaam Hong Kong Karachi
Kuala Lumpur Madrid Melbourne Mexico City Nairobi
New Delhi Shanghai Taipei Toronto
With offices in
Argentina Austria Brazil Chile Czech Republic France Greece
Guatemala Hungary Italy Japan South Korea Poland Portugal
Singapore Switzerland Thailand Turkey Ukraine Vietnam

OXFORD is a trademark of Oxford University Press.

ISBN-13: 978-0-19-435073-0
ISBN-10: 0-19-435073-8

Copyright © 1999 Oxford University Press

No unauthorized photocopying.

All rights reserved. No part of this publication may be
reproduced, stored in a retrieval system, or transmitted, in any
form or by any means, electronic, mechanical, photocopying,
recording, or otherwise, without the prior written permission of
Oxford University Press.

This book is sold subject to the condition that it shall not, by
way of trade or otherwise, be lent, resold, hired out, or
otherwise circulated without the publisher's prior consent in any
form of binding or cover other than that in which it is published
and without a similar condition including this condition being
imposed on the subsequent purchaser.

Editorial Manager: Susan Lanzano
Editor: Lynne Barsky
Production Editor: Klaus Jekeli
Art Director: Lynn Luchetti
Design Project Manager: Susan Brorein
Designer: Shelley Himmelstein
Art Buyer: Patricia Marx
Cover design production: Brett Sonnenschein
Picture Researcher: Clare Maxwell
Production Manager: Abram Hall
Cover design by Silver Editions

Printing (last digit): 20 19 18 17 16 15 14 13 12 11

Printed in China

Illustrations, realia, and handwriting by: Gary Antonetti/Ortelius
Design, Craig Attebery, Eliot Bergman, Annie Bissett, Carlos
Castellanos, Jim DeLapine, Marcia Hartsock, Shelley
Himmelstein, Pamela Johnson, Claudia C. Kehrhahn, Uldis
Klavins, MacNeill & Macintosh/Scott MacNeill, Mohammad
Mansoor, Mary Chandler, Karen Minot, Irena Roman/Deborah
Wolfe Ltd., Stacey Schuett, Carol L. Strebel, Bill Thomson, Anna
Veltfort, Nina Wallace

Location and studio photography by: Stephen Ogilvy

*The publishers would like to thank the following for their
permission to reproduce photographs:* Cafe Biondi; Ron
Chapple, Jim Cummings, Robert Hager, Michael Keller,
Frederick McKinney/FPG; Michael Justice, Bob Schatz/Liaison
International; Frans Lanting/Minden Pictures; Tony
Freeman/Photo Edit; Ken Cavanagh, Renee Lynn, Rafael Macia,
David Weintraub/Photo Researchers; Rob Lewine, Don Mason,
Roy Morsch/The Stock Market; Glen Allison, Warren Bolster,
Cosmo Condina, Darrell Fulin, Lori Adamski Peek, Thomas J.
Peterson, Fritz Prenzel, Colin Prior, Tom Ulrich/Tony Stone
Images; Spalding; Bachmann, C. Yarbrough/Uniphoto; AP/Wide
World Photo

Acknowledgments

The publisher and author would like to thank the following reviewers for their help throughout the development of the workbooks:

Glenda Adamson, Lubie G. Alatriste, Leor Alcalay, Fiona Armstrong, Jean Barlow, Margrajean Bonilla, Susan Burke, Becky Carle, Bev Clausner, Analee Doney, Laurie Ehrenhalt, Michele Epstein, Christine Evans, Lynn A. Freeland, Carole Goodman, Joyce Grabowski, Esther Greenwell, Kelly Gutierrez, Christine Hill, Leann Howard, Lori Howard, Hilary Jarvis, Nanette Kafka, Cliff Ker, Margaret Lombard, Carol S. McLain, Monica Miele, Patsy Mills, Debra L. Mullins, Dian Perkins, Barbara Jane Pers, Marianne Riggiola, Virginia Robbins, Linda Susan Robinson, Michele Rodgers-Amini, Maria Salinas, Jimmy E. Sandifer, Jeffrey Scofield, Ann Silverman, Susan A. Slavin, Peggy Stubbs, Lynn Sweeden, Christine Tierney, Laura L. Webber

In addition, the author would like to thank the following people:

Susan Lanzano, Editorial Manager, for overseeing a huge and complex project of which the *Workbooks* were just a part. She orchestrated the entire project without losing sight of the individual components.

Lynne Barsky, Editor, for four years of hard work and dedication, from the all-important initial research to the scrutinizing of final copy and art. I appreciate Lynne's calm and upbeat steadfastness throughout the project.

Klaus Jekeli, Production Editor, for applying his intelligent, keen eye to the manuscript and art, assuring that everything worked together.

Norma Shapiro and Jayme Adelson-Goldstein, authors of the *Dictionary,* and Shirley Brod, editor of the *Teacher's Book,* for meticulously reviewing the manuscript and offering particularly helpful feedback and enthusiastic support.

Eliza Jensen and Amy Cooper, senior editors, for looking at the manuscript at important junctures and offering sage advice.

Margo Bonner, my coauthor of the *Intermediate Workbook,* for her very valuable feedback during the developmental phase of this project and for her insightful critique of the manuscript.

The design team for making me feel welcome at their meetings, and for giving me the chance to see the huge amount of work and creativity they put into the project long after the manuscript had been submitted.

Rick Smith, as always, for his unswerving support and for his insightful comments on all aspects of the project. Once again, he proved to be equally at home in both the world of numbers and the world of words.

To the Teacher

The *Beginning Workbook* and the *Intermediate Workbook* that accompany *The Oxford Picture Dictionary* have been designed to provide meaningful and enjoyable practice of the vocabulary that students are learning. These workbooks supply high-interest contexts and real information for enrichment and self-expression.

Both *Workbooks* conveniently correspond page-for-page to the 140 topics of the *Picture Dictionary*. For example, if you are working on page 22 in the *Dictionary,* the activities for this topic, Age and Physical Description, will be found on page 22 in the *Workbook.*

All topics in the *Beginning Workbook* follow the same easy-to-use format. Exercise 1 is always a "look in your dictionary" activity where students are asked to complete a task while looking in their *Picture Dictionary*. The tasks include answering questions about the pictures, judging statements true or false, counting the number of illustrated occurrences of a vocabulary item, completing a time line, or speculating about who said what.

Following this activity are one or more content-rich contextualized exercises, including true or false, matching, labeling, fill-in-the-blanks, multiple choice, rank ordering, categorizing, odd-one-out, and completion of forms. These exercises often feature graphs and charts with real data for students to work with as they practice the new vocabulary. Many topics include a personalization exercise that asks "What about you?" where students can use the new vocabulary to give information about their own lives or to express their opinions.

The final exercise for each topic is a "Challenge" which can be assigned to students for additional work in class or as homework. Challenge activities provide higher level speaking and writing practice, and for some topics will require students to interview classmates, conduct surveys, or find information outside of class. For example on page 37, the Challenge for the topic Apartments asks students to look at a local newspaper, choose an apartment ad, and describe the apartment.

Each of the 12 units ends with "Another Look," a review which allows students to practice vocabulary from all of the topics of a unit in a game or puzzle-like activity, such as picture crosswords, word searches, and C-searches, where students search in a picture for items which begin with the letter *c*. These activities are at the back of the *Beginning Workbook* on pages 170–181.

Throughout both the *Beginning* and the *Intermediate Workbooks,* vocabulary is carefully controlled and recycled. Students should, however, be encouraged to use their *Picture Dictionaries* to look up words that they do not recall or, if they are doing topics out of sequence, may not yet have learned.

The *Oxford Picture Dictionary Workbooks* can be used in the classroom or at home for self-study. A separate *Answer Key* with the answers to both *Workbooks* is available.

I hope you and your students enjoy using these workbooks as much as I have enjoyed writing them.

M.F.

To the Student

The Oxford Picture Dictionary has more than 3,700 words. This workbook will help you use them in your daily life.

• It's easy to use! The *Workbook* pages match the pages in your *Picture Dictionary*. For example, to practice the words on page 22 in your *Picture Dictionary*, go to page 22 in your *Workbook*.

• It has exercises you will enjoy. Some exercises show real information. A bar graph of people's favorite colors is on page 12, and a chart showing the top 10 pets in the United States is on page 133. Another exercise, which asks "What about you?" gives you a chance to use your

own information. You'll find stories, puzzles, and conversations, too.

At the end of each topic there is a Challenge, a chance to use your new vocabulary more independently. And finally, every unit has a one-page summary, called Another Look, in a section at the back of the book. This is a game or puzzle activity that practices the vocabulary from an entire unit.

Learning new words is both challenging and fun. I had a lot of fun writing this workbook. I hope you enjoy using it!

M.F.

Contents

1. Everyday Language

2. People

3. Housing

4. Food

Contents

10. Plants and Animals

11. Work

12. Recreation

A Classroom

1. Look at the classroom in your dictionary. How many ... are there?

   a. teachers   <u> 1 </u>   **c.** students   <u>   </u>   **e.** globes   <u>   </u>

   b. computers   <u>   </u>   **d.** cassette players <u>   </u>   **f.** maps   <u>   </u>

2. Look at the list of school supplies. Check (✓) the items you see on the table.

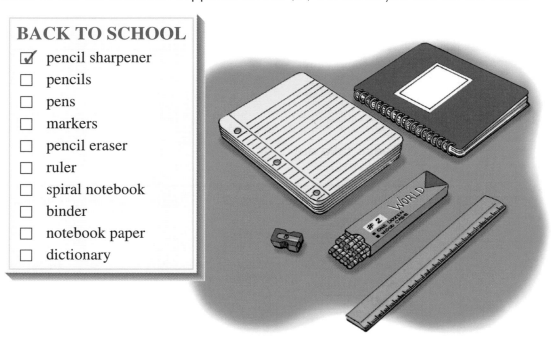

BACK TO SCHOOL

- ☑ pencil sharpener
- ☐ pencils
- ☐ pens
- ☐ markers
- ☐ pencil eraser
- ☐ ruler
- ☐ spiral notebook
- ☐ binder
- ☐ notebook paper
- ☐ dictionary

3. Correct this student's spelling test.

> *Spelling Test*
>
> 1. screen   6. eraser
>
> 2. overhead pro*j*ector   7. alfabet
>
> 3. computter   8. map
>
> 4. clock   9. bookkase
>
> 5. chawk   10. bulletin bord

4. Match the instructions with the pictures. Write the number.

_8_ **a.** Listen to the cassette.

___ **b.** Open your workbooks.

___ **c.** Write the numbers on the board.

___ **d.** Please stand up.

___ **e.** Please take out your pencils.

___ **f.** Erase the chalkboard, please.

___ **g.** Please close your workbooks.

___ **h.** Put away your pencils.

___ **i.** Please take a seat.

___ **j.** Write the alphabet on the board.

1.

2.

3.

4.

5.

6.

7.

8.

9.

10.

5. What about you? Check (✓) the items you use in your classroom.

☐ pencils   ☐ dictionary   ☐ notebook paper

☐ pens   ☐ picture dictionary   ☐ binder

☐ markers   ☐ spiral notebook   ☐ ruler

☐ pencil sharpener   ☐ workbook   ☐ cassette player

☐ pencil eraser   ☐ textbook   ☐ Other: _____

Challenge Write about the items in Exercise 5. **Example:** *I have one dictionary. I have two pens. I don't have any pencils.*

3

Personal Information

1. Look in your dictionary. What is Sam Larson's...?

   a. ZIP code ____11364____   **c.** apartment # _____

   b. area code _____   **d.** Social Security # _____

2. Match the personal information words with the examples. Write the number.

   _6_ **a.** middle initial   **1.** female

   ____ **b.** signature   **2.** California

   ____ **c.** city   **3.** (310)

   ____ **d.** sex   **4.** 123-45-6789

   ____ **e.** area code   **5.** Los Angeles

   ____ **f.** Social Security number **6.** S.

   ____ **g.** name   **7.** 90049

   ____ **h.** ZIP code   **8.** *Miriam S. Shakter*

   ____ **i.** state   **9.** Miriam S. Shakter

3. What about you? Fill out the form. Use your own information.

   Last name_____ First name_____ Middle initial_____

   Sex ☐ male ☐ female

   Place of birth_____ Date of birth_____
                                              (month)   (date)   (year)

   Address_____ Apt. #_____

   _____
   (city)   (state)   (ZIP code)

   Telephone (_____) _____

   _____   _____
   Signature   Social Security #

Challenge Interview a classmate. Find out his or her last name, first name, middle initial, address, and place of birth. Write the information on your own paper.

1. Look in your dictionary. Put the words in the correct column.

PEOPLE	PLACES	
teacher	_classroom_	

2. Look at the floor plan. Complete the directory.

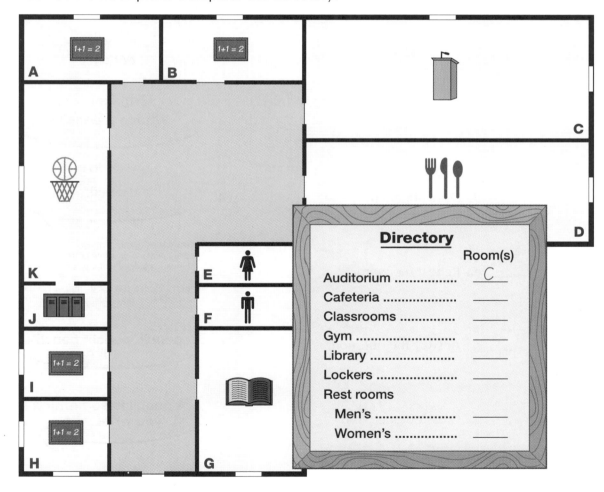

Directory

	Room(s)
Auditorium	_C_
Cafeteria	
Classrooms	
Gym	
Library	
Lockers	
Rest rooms	
Men's	
Women's	

3. What about you? Check (✓) the items your school has.

☐ an auditorium   ☐ a library   ☐ a track   ☐ a counselor's office   ☐ a cafeteria

Challenge Draw a floor plan or write a directory for your school.

1. Look in your dictionary. **True** or **False**?
   a. **Picture A:** The woman is dictating a sentence. _____False_____
   b. **Picture I:** The men are sharing a book. _____
   c. **Picture K:** The group is discussing a story. _____
   d. **Picture P:** The students are talking with each other. _____
   e. **Picture Q:** The student is correcting papers. _____

2. Match the instructions with the responses. Write the number.

   _3_ a. Ask a question.

   1. P - E - N - C - I - L

   ___ b. Copy the word.

   2. *pencil*
      pencil

   ___ c. Say the word.

   3. What's a pencil?

   ___ d. Draw a pencil.

   4. Pencil.

   ___ e. Repeat the word.

   5. **pence** /pens/ *n.* (*pl.*) pennies.
      pencil /ˈpensl/ *n.* instrument for writing and drawing, made of a thin piece of wood with lead inside it.
      penetrate /ˈpenɪtreɪt/ *v.* go into or through something: *A nail penetrated the car tire.*

   ___ f. Answer the question.

   6. pencil pencil pencil

   ___ g. Cross out the word.

   7. A pencil is something you write with.

   ___ h. Look up the word.

   8. [drawing of a pencil]

   ___ i. Spell the word.

   9. ~~pencil~~

3. Complete this test.

Name:_____   Class: _____

1. Fill in the blanks. Use the words in the box.

~~in~~   out   up

a. I'm filling ___in___ the blanks.

b. The students are looking _____ new words in the dictionary.

c. The teacher is passing _____ the papers.

2. Cross out the word that doesn't belong.

a. help   share   ~~match~~

b. spell   underline   circle

c. draw   talk   copy

3. Underline the words that begin with *s*. Circle the words that begin with *c*.

read   (copy)   _say_   share   help   circle   check   spell

4. Put the words in question 3 in alphabetical order.

___check_____

_____

_____

_____

_____

_____

_____

_____

5. Match.

_3_ **a.** Spell   **1.** a picture.

____ **b.** Draw   **2.** a question

____ **c.** Ask   **3.** a word.

4. What about you? Look in your dictionary. Which classroom activities do you like? Which activities don't you like? Make two lists on your own paper.

Challenge Look up the word *thimble* in your picture dictionary.

a. Write the word: _____   **c.** Draw a picture of a thimble.

b. Write the page number: _____

Everyday Conversation

1. Look in your dictionary. Match the parts of the conversations. Write the number.

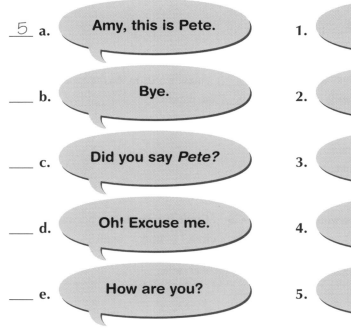

5 a.   Amy, this is Pete.

___ b.   Bye.

___ c.   Did you say *Pete?*

___ d.   Oh! Excuse me.

___ e.   How are you?

1.   OK, thanks.

2.   See you.

3.   I'm sorry.

4.   Yes, Pete.

5.   Hi, Pete.

2. Circle the correct words.

a. John introduces his friend:

Hello.

Hi, I'm Ming.

(Ming, this is Kim.)

b. Ming makes sure he understands:

Oh! Excuse me.

How are things?

Did you say *Kim?*

c. Ming begins a conversation:

See you.

Good night.

How are things?

d. John compliments Ming:

That's a great jacket.

See you.

Thank you.

e. Ming thanks John:

I'm sorry.

Thank you.

Fine, thanks.

f. Ming ends the conversation:

Good evening.

Good morning.

See you.

Challenge Look at **page 182** in this book. Complete the conversation.

1. Look in your dictionary. Match the numbers with the words.

_4_ **a.** 555-2134   **1.** long-distance call

___ **b.** 1 (401) 543-4323   **2.** emergency service

___ **c.** 411   **3.** operator

___ **d.** 0   **4.** local call

___ **e.** 011-57-1-555-3456   **5.** directory assistance

___ **f.** 911   **6.** international call

2. Put the sentences in the correct order. Then fill in the blank.

> **Instructions for a _____ phone**
>
> ____ **a.** Listen for the dial tone.   ____ **d.** Deposit coins.
>
> _1_ **b.** Pick up the receiver.   ____ **e.** Hang up the receiver.
>
> ____ **c.** Leave a message.   ____ **f.** Dial the number.

3. Complete the ad. Use the words in the box.

> answering machine
> cellular phone
> cordless phone
> pager
> ~~phone~~

The Busy Signal

SAVE! SAVE! SAVE!

~~$29.99~~ $19.99

~~$44.99~~ $24.99

a. _phone_
black, white, beige

b. _____

~~$139.99~~ $99.99

~~$109.99~~ $69.99

~~$69.99~~ $49.99
25-Channel

c. _____   **d.** _____   **e.** _____

4. What about you? Complete the phone numbers for your city or town.

Important Numbers

Emergency service: _____

Non-emergency service: _____

Directory Assistance (local calls): _____

Long Distance Operator: _____

Challenge Find out the area codes for five cities. Look in a phone book or ask your classmates.
Example: *Houston—713*

Weather

1. Look in your dictionary. Describe the temperature.

   a. Fahrenheit: 95° ___hot___   35° _____   60° _____

   b. Celsius: 25° _____   -10° _____   40° _____

2. Look at the weather map. Check (✔) the statements that are true.

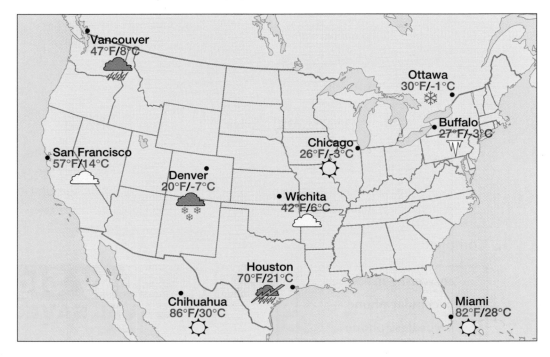

☐ **a.** It's raining in San Francisco.

☑ **b.** There's a snowstorm in Denver.

☐ **c.** Houston is having a hailstorm.

☐ **d.** It's clear in Chihuahua.

☐ **e.** It's freezing in Ottawa.

☐ **f.** It's snowing in Vancouver.

☐ **g.** It's icy in Buffalo.

☐ **h.** It's sunny but freezing in Chicago.

☐ **i.** It's hot and sunny in Miami.

☐ **j.** It's cloudy and warm in Wichita.

3. What about you? What kinds of weather do you like? Check (✔) the columns.

	I LIKE IT	IT'S OK	I DON'T LIKE IT
humid			
cool and foggy			
rainy			
warm and windy			
Other: _____			

Challenge Write a weather report for your city. **Example:** *Monday, January 25. Today it's sunny and warm in San Antonio. The temperature is…*

1. Look in your dictionary. Write the opposites.

    a. big   _little_   **d.** cheap   _____

    b. fat   _____   **e.** ugly   _____

    c. heavy   _____   **f.** slow   _____

2. Look at the picture of the classroom.

True or **False**? Change the underlined words in the false sentences. Make the sentences true.

    a. The classroom is noisy.   _False. The classroom is quiet._

    b. There's a big clock in the room.   _____

    c. Bob is a good student.   _____

    d. The teacher's desk is messy.   _____

    e. The bookcase is neat.   _____

    f. The words on the board are easy.   _____

    g. The chairs are soft.   _____

3. What about you? Check (✔) the words that describe your classroom.

    ☐ beautiful   ☐ big   ☐ cold   ☐ hot   ☐ messy

    ☐ neat   ☐ noisy   ☐ quiet   ☐ ugly   ☐ Other: _____

Challenge   Describe your classroom. Write eight sentences.

Colors

1. Look at **page 3** in your dictionary. What color is the…?

    a. binder   <u>green</u>   **c.** textbook   _____

    b. spiral notebook   _____   **d.** ruler   _____

2. Look at the bar graph. Put the colors in order. (Number 1 = their favorite)

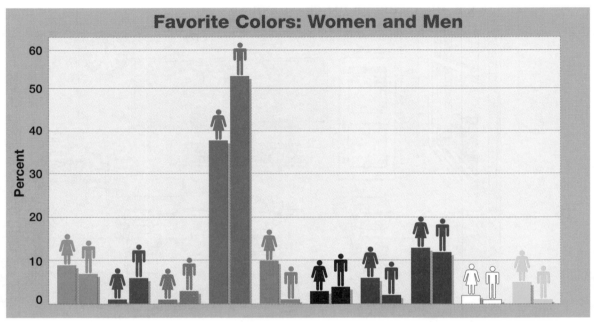

Based on information from: Weiss, D.: *The Great Divide: How Females & Males Really Differ.*
(NY: Poseidon Press, 1991)

WOMEN'S FAVORITE COLORS	MEN'S FAVORITE COLORS
1. <u>blue</u>	**1.** _____
2. _____	**2.** _____
3. _____	**3.** _____
4. _____	**4.** _____
5. _____	**5.** _____
6. _____	**6.** _____
7. _____	**7.** _____
8. _____	**8.** _____, _____, and _____
9. _____ and _____	

3. What about you? Put the colors in order. (Number 1 = your favorite)

    ___ red   ___ green   ___ purple   ___ light blue   ___ orange

    ___ yellow   ___ pink   ___ brown   ___ dark blue   ___ beige

Challenge   Make a list of the colors in Exercise 2. Ask five women and five men to put the colors in order. (Number 1 = their favorite) Do their answers agree with the information in Exercise 2?

Colors

1. Look in your dictionary. **True** or **False**?

    a. The black box is on a shelf.   _True_

    b. The white box is under the black box.   _____

    c. The purple box is next to the pink box.   _____

    d. The gray box is behind the turquoise box.   _____

    e. The red box is near the yellow box.   _____

2. Follow the instructions below.

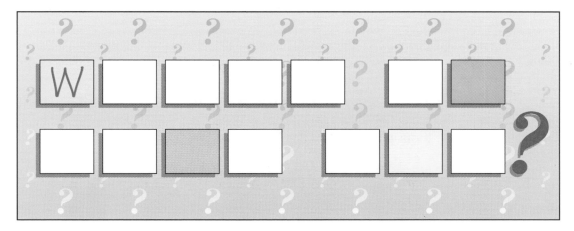

    a. Put the letter **W** in the pink box.

    b. Put a **Y** below it.

    c. Put an **E** in the yellow box.

    d. Put an **I** above it.

    e. Put a **P** next to the **E,** on the left.

    f. Put a **U** in the green box.

    g. Put an **O** between the **Y** and the **U.**

    h. Put an **E** above the **U.**

    i. Put an **R** next to the **U,** on the right.

    j. Put an **H** between the **W** and the **E.**

Now, put the letters **E, N, R,** and **S** in the correct boxes to complete the question.

3. What about you? Look at Exercise 2. Answer the question.

_____

Challenge   Draw a picture of your classroom. Write about the locations of the classroom items in
your picture. **Example:** _The map is next to the board, on the right._

Numbers and Measurements

1. Look in your dictionary. What kinds of numbers are these?

   a. thirty ___cardinal___   c. III _____   e. 3% _____

   b. 1/3 _____   d. thirteenth _____   f. thirteen _____

2. Complete the chart.

WORD	NUMBER	ROMAN NUMERAL
ten	10	X
		III
	15	
		L
	20	
one hundred		
		D
one thousand		

3. Look at the bar graph. Ana is first (= the best) in her class. What about the other students? Complete the sentences.

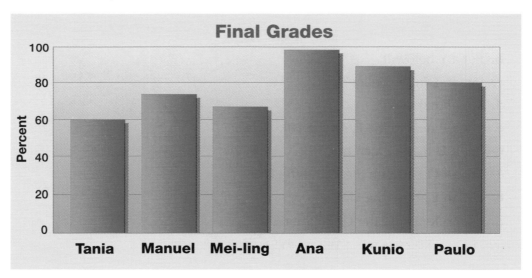

Final Grades

a. Ana is ___first___ in her class.   d. Kunio is _____.

b. Manuel is _____.   e. Tania is _____.

c. Mei-ling is _____.   f. Paulo is _____.

4. Complete the pie chart with numbers from the box. Then complete the sentences. Write the percents in words.

| ~~50~~ | 25 | 10 | 10 | 5 |

First Languages in Mrs. Rivera's Class
(Percentage of Students)

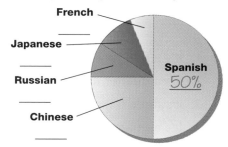

a. ___Fifty percent___ speak Spanish.

b. _____ speak Chinese.

c. _____ speak French.

d. _____ speak Russian.

e. _____ speak Japanese.

5. Look at the books. Complete the sentences. Use fractions in words.

a. ___One-fourth___ of the books are in Chinese.

b. _____ are in English.

c. _____ are in Spanish.

d. _____ are in either English or Russian.

6. What about you? Measure a bookshelf in school or at home. Complete the chart.

	FEET AND INCHES	METERS AND CENTIMETERS
width		
height		
depth		

Challenge How many students in your class speak your language? How many students speak other languages? Calculate the percents. **Example:** *There are twenty students in my class. Ten students speak Spanish. That's fifty percent.*

Time

1. Look in your dictionary. What's another way to say…?

   a. ten-thirty   _half past ten_   **c.** a quarter after three _____

   b. two forty-five _____   **d.** twenty after six _____

2. Match the numbers with the words.

   _3_ **a.** 3:00
   ___ **b.** 5:25
   ___ **c.** 2:30
   ___ **d.** 6:45
   ___ **e.** 8:50
   ___ **f.** 6:15
   ___ **g.** 9:10
   ___ **h.** 5:45

   1. It's ten to nine.
   2. It's a quarter to seven.
   3. It's three o'clock.
   4. It's a quarter past six.
   5. It's a quarter to six.
   6. It's two-thirty.
   7. It's five twenty-five.
   8. It's ten after nine.

3. Complete the clocks.

   ```
   4:10        :           :           :
   ```

   a. ten after four   **b.** half past six   **c.** eight o'clock   **d.** a quarter to twelve

4. What about you? Answer the questions. Use words and numbers.

   Example: What time is it? It's _four-fifteen p.m. (4:15 p.m.)_ .

   a. What time is it? It's _____ (_____) .

   b. What time is your class? From _____ (_____) to
   _____ (_____) .

5. Look in your dictionary. In which time zone is…?

    a. Caracas   <u>Atlantic</u>   **c.** Denver   _____

    b. Chicago   _____   **d.** Vancouver _____

6. Look at the chart.

At 12:00 noon, Eastern Standard Time, the time in … is …

Athens	7 P.M.	**Mexico City**	11 A.M.
Baghdad	8 P.M.	**Montreal**	12 N
Bangkok	12 M	**New York City**	12 N
Barcelona	6 P.M.	**Panama**	12 N
Buenos Aires	2 P.M.	**Paris**	6 P.M.
Calcutta	10:30 P.M.	**Rio de Janeiro**	2 P.M.
Frankfurt	6 P.M.	**Riyadh**	8 P.M.
Halifax	1 P.M.	**Rome**	6 P.M.
Hanoi	1 A.M.*	**St. Petersburg**	8 P.M.
Havana	12 N	**San Juan**	12 N
Hong Kong	1 A.M.*	**Seoul**	2 A.M.*
Houston	11 A.M.	**Sydney**	3 A.M.*
London	5 P.M.	**Tel Aviv**	7 P.M.
Los Angeles	9 A.M.	**Tokyo**	2 A.M.*
Mecca	8 P.M.	**Zurich**	6 P.M.

* = the next day   M = midnight   N = noon

It's noon in New York. What time is it in…? Use numbers and the words in the box.

in the morning   **in the afternoon**   **in the evening**
at night   **noon**   **midnight**

    a. Athens   <u>7:00 in the evening</u>   **g.** St. Petersburg _____

    b. London   _____   **h.** Bangkok   _____

    c. Calcutta   _____   **i.** Mexico City _____

    d. Panama   _____   **j.** Frankfurt   _____

    e. Halifax   _____   **k.** Los Angeles _____

    f. Tokyo   _____   **l.** Hanoi   _____

7. What about you? Does your country have…? Write **Yes** or **No.**

    a. different time zones   _____   **b.** daylight saving time   _____

Challenge Look in your dictionary. Which cities from the chart in Exercise 6 are in the eight time zones pictured? List them for each zone. **Example:** *eastern time: Havana, Montreal,…*

The Calendar

1. Look in your dictionary. In January, 2001, how many … are there?

    a. days   <u>31</u>   **d.** weekdays   _____

    b. Mondays   _____   **e.** weekends   _____

    c. Thursdays   _____   **f.** full weeks   _____

2. Look at Antonio's calendar. **True** or **False**?

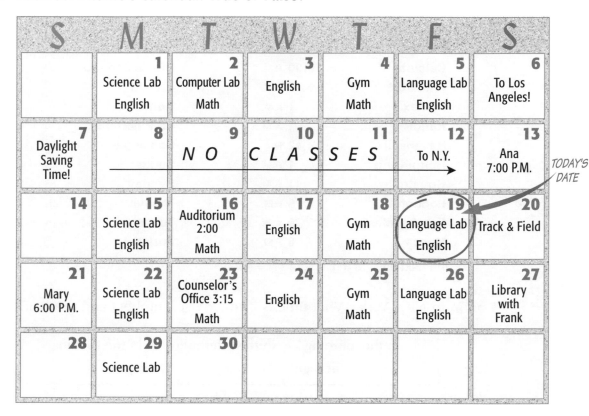

    a. Antonio has class every day this month.   <u>False</u>

    b. He has English twice a week.   _____

    c. He was in New York last weekend.   _____

    d. Tomorrow he has track and field.   _____

    e. Yesterday was Tuesday.   _____

    f. He sees Mary Sunday night.   _____

    g. He sees her every weekend.   _____

    h. There were no classes last week.   _____

    i. Daylight saving time begins this week.   _____

    j. Next week Antonio sees the school counselor. _____

3. What about you? Make a calendar of <u>your</u> monthly activities. Write ten sentences.

4. Put these months in the correct seasons. Use your dictionary for help.

~~April~~ October January February
November July May August

WINTER	SPRING	SUMMER	FALL
	April		

5. Match the photos with the captions. Write the letter.

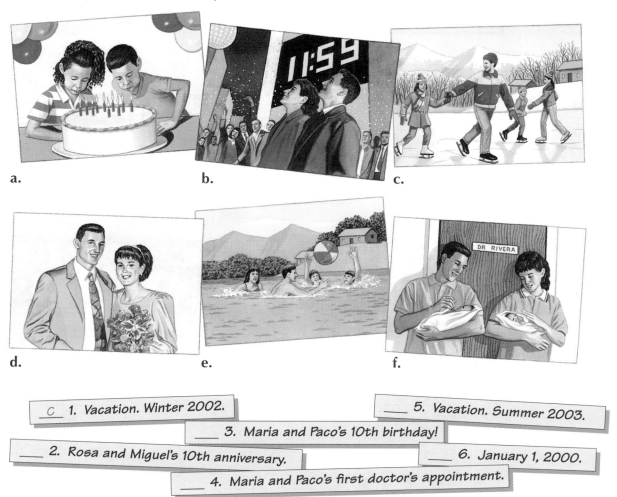

a.

b.

c.

d.

e.

f.

_C_ 1. Vacation. Winter 2002.

___ 5. Vacation. Summer 2003.

___ 3. Maria and Paco's 10th birthday!

___ 2. Rosa and Miguel's 10th anniversary.

___ 6. January 1, 2000.

___ 4. Maria and Paco's first doctor's appointment.

6. What about you? Complete the chart on your own paper.

	BIRTHDAY		ANNIVERSARY	
	MONTH	DAY	MONTH	DAY
Your name: _____				
Classmate's name: _____				
Classmate's name: _____				

Challenge   Bring some photos to class. Write captions on your own paper.

Money

1. Look in your dictionary. How much money is there in…? (Do not include **Ways to pay.**)

   a. coins ___$1.91___ b. bills _____ c. coins and bills _____

2. Look at the money. How much is it? Use numbers.

   a. ___$5.10___

   b. $ _____ or _____ ¢

   c. _____ or _____

   d. _____

   e. _____

   f. _____

3. You borrowed $25.00 from Mary Johnson. Pay her back.

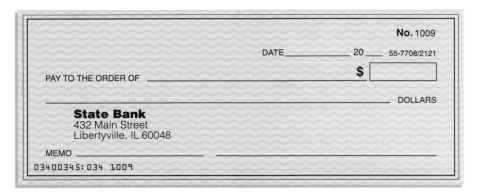

   Check (✓) the form of payment.

   ☐ cash   ☐ traveler's check   ☐ personal check   ☐ money order

Challenge Look at **page 182** in this book. Answer the questions.

1. Look in your dictionary. Circle the correct words to complete the sentences.

  a. The woman is shopping for <u>two /(three)</u> sweaters.

  b. The <u>regular price/ sale price</u> is $9.99.

  c. The <u>change / total</u> is $32.44.

  d. There <u>is / is no</u> sales tax.

  e. The woman <u>gives / sells</u> the sweaters to her daughters.

  f. One of the daughters <u>returns / keeps</u> the red sweater.

  g. One of the daughters exchanges the <u>blue / green</u> sweater.

2. Complete the shopping tips. Use the words in the box.

change	exchange	keep	pay	price
~~receipt~~	return	sales		

BE A $MART $HOPPER

✶ Check the price .

✶ Get a ___receipt___ .
   a.

   Is the _____ on the receipt correct?
   b.

   Is the _____ tax correct?
   c.

✶ If you _____ by cash, count your _____ .
   d.   **e.**

✶ Ask:

   Can I _____ this for something else?
   f.

   Can I _____ this for cash?
   g.

✶ _____ your receipt.
   h.

3. What about you? Is there sales tax on clothing in your state? _____
   If yes, how much is it? _____%

Challenge Look at **page 183** in this book. Complete the sales slip.

▶ **Go to page 170 for Another Look (Unit 1).**

Age and Physical Description

1. Look at the top of the page in your dictionary. How many ... do you see?

   a. people __9__   **b.** children _____   **c.** teenagers _____   **d.** adults _____

2. Read the ads. Circle all the words that describe age and physical description. Who wrote the ads? Match the ads with the photos. Write the letter.

(Tall) and (Attractive)—middle-aged man of (average weight) seeks friend for travel and sports.
_c_ **1.** 3759 ✉ ☎

Attractive—slim, elderly woman with many interests seeks relationship with kind, honest man. 3145 ☎
____ **2.**

Hi!—I'm a short, cute, 30-year-old woman. You're smart, nice, and funny. Physical appearance not important. 3945 ✉
____ **3.**

Short and Sweet—18-year-old of average weight seeks nice fun-loving man. Photo please. 3296 ✉ ☎
____ **4.**

Something Special—I'm a young, physically challenged man looking for someone to share the great things in life with. 3623 ☎
____ **5.**

A Great Guy—heavyset, friendly and fun. Looking for a happy woman who loves life. 3567 ✉ ☎
____ **6.**

a.   **b.**

c.   **d.**

e.   **f.**

3. What about you? Describe one of your friends. Circle the correct words.

My friend's name is _____.

		short	thin	young	man.
He's	a	average height	average weight	middle-aged	woman.
She's	an	tall	heavyset	elderly	boy.
					girl.

Challenge   Find a picture of a person in a newspaper, magazine, or your dictionary. Write a description.

22

1. Look at the top picture in your dictionary. How many ... do you see?

a. green rollers ___2___   d. brushes _____

b. combs _____   e. hair stylists _____

c. blow dryers _____   f. scissors _____

2. Look at the pictures of Cindi. Check (✓) the things that The Hair Salon did to Cindi's hair. Then circle the correct words to complete the paragraph.

Before

Now

The Hair Salon

- ☑ cut
- ☐ set
- ☐ color
- ☐ perm

Cindi is very happy with her new hair

style. She now has long / (short)
                              a.

straight / wavy, brown / blond hair. She
          b.   **c.**

also has a part / bangs. Cindi looks great.
              d.

3. What about you? Draw a picture of a friend's hair. Describe it.

Example:

My friend has ___shoulder-length__, ____curly_____,

_____red_____ hair.

My friend has _____, _____,

_____ hair.

Check (✓) the correct boxes. He/she has....

☐ a part   ☐ bangs   ☐ a mustache   ☐ a beard   ☐ sideburns

Challenge Find pictures of three hair styles in a newspaper, magazine, or your dictionary. Write descriptions.

Family

1. Look at page 24 in your dictionary. Put the words in the correct category.

brother	cousin	daughter	grandmother
husband	niece	parent	son uncle

MALE	FEMALE	MALE OR FEMALE
brother	_____	_____
_____	_____	_____
_____	_____	
_____		

2. Look at page 24 in your dictionary. **True** or **False**?

a. Tom has two sisters.   False

b. Min is Lu's wife.   _____

c. Daniel is Min and Lu's nephew.   _____

d. Tom and Emily have the same grandparents.   _____

e. Rose is Emily's aunt.   _____

f. Marta is Eddie's mother-in-law.   _____

g. Sara is Berta and Mario's granddaughter.   _____

h. Felix is Alice's cousin.   _____

i. Ana is Carlos's sister-in-law.   _____

j. Tito is Berta and Mario's son-in-law.   _____

3. What about you? Complete the form.

Your name:_____

Mother's name:_____ Father's name:_____

Marital status: ☐ single ☐ married ☐ divorced

If married, what is your husband's/wife's name?_____

Do you have any children? ☐ yes ☐ no

If yes, what are their names?_____

4. Look at page 25 in your dictionary. Circle the correct answer.

   a. Carol is Dan's (former wife)/ sister.

   b. Sue is Kim's <u>stepmother / mother</u>.

   c. Rick is a <u>single father / father</u>.

   d. David is Mary's <u>brother / half brother</u>.

   e. Lisa is Bill's <u>half sister / stepsister</u>.

   f. Dan is Bill and Kim's <u>father / stepfather</u>.

5. Look at Megan's story.

Put these sentences about Megan in the correct time order.

____ She's remarried.   ____ She's a stepmother.   _1_ She's married.

____ She has a baby.   ____ She's a single mother.   ____ She's divorced.

6. Complete Nicole's story. Use the information in Exercise 5.

Sept. 10, 2002

Name: *Nicole Parker*

My name is Nicole. My ____mother____'s name is Megan.
                                  a.

My _____'s name is Chet. I have a _____.
         b.   c.

His name is Brian. Brian has a _____.
                                   d.

His name is Jason. Jason is my_____.
                                 e.

Challenge Draw your family tree. Use the family trees in your dictionary as a model.

Daily Routines

1. Look in your dictionary. Complete Dan Lim's schedule.

6:00	wake up
	get dressed
7:00	
7:30	
	drive to work
5:00	
	pick up the children
	have dinner
8:00	
8:30	
	go to sleep

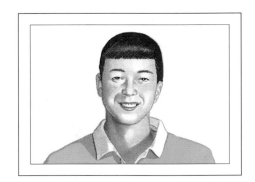

2. Look at the Lims' things. Match each item with the correct activity. Write the letter.

To Do

_f_ 1. go to the market

___ 2. clean the house

___ 3. take the bus

___ 4. make lunch

___ 5. watch TV

___ 6. read the paper

___ 7. do homework

3. Read about Nora Lim. Complete the story. Use the words in the boxes.

eats	gets up	~~relaxes~~	takes

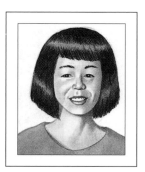

Nora Lim has a busy week. Sundays are busy, too, but she

_____relaxes_____ a little more. She _____ at
        a.   **b.**

8:00 and _____ a long, hot shower. Then
                  c.

she _____ breakfast with her family.
        d.

drives	goes	leaves	makes	picks up

After breakfast she _____ her husband to the shoe store. Then she
                           e.

takes the children to their Aunt Ellen. Ellen _____ lunch for them.
                                            f.

After lunch, Nora _____ Ellen's house and _____ to
                     g.   **h.**

the library for two hours. At 4:00 she _____ the children from Ellen's.
                                            i.

eats	gets	goes	makes	takes	watches

Nora _____ home at 5:00 and _____ dinner. Her
           j.   **k.**

daughter, Sara, helps her. Dan _____ the bus home. The family
                              l.

_____ dinner at 6:00. They talk about their day. After dinner, Nora
        m.

_____ TV with her family. At 10:00 Nora _____ to bed.
        n.   **o.**

4. What about you? Complete your weekday or weekend schedule. Use your own paper. Use the schedule in Exercise 1 as an example.

Challenge Interview someone you know (a friend, family member, or classmate). Write a schedule of his or her daily routine.

Life Events

1. Look in your dictionary. Complete the time line for Martin Perez.

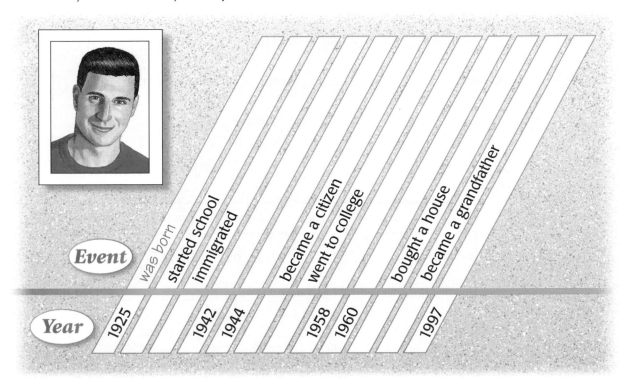

Event was born | started school | immigrated | became a citizen | went to college | bought a house | became a grandfather

Year 1925 | | 1942 | 1944 | 1958 | 1960 | 1997

2. Complete the story about Rosa Lopez. Use the words in the box.

~~was~~	died	fell	got	got
graduated	had	learned	moved	rented

Rosa Lopez _____was_____ born in the United States
                    a.

in 1928. She _____ from high school in 1945.
                      b.

In 1946 she _____ to drive and
                    c.

_____ to California. She _____
        d.   **e.**

a job and _____ an apartment with a friend.
                  f.

Then she met Martin. They _____ in love, _____
                                g.   **h.**

married, and _____ two children. They were very happy until Martin
                    i.

_____ in 1997. Today Rosa lives in Florida with her daughter and
      j.

grandchildren.

3. Match the words with the pictures. Write the number.

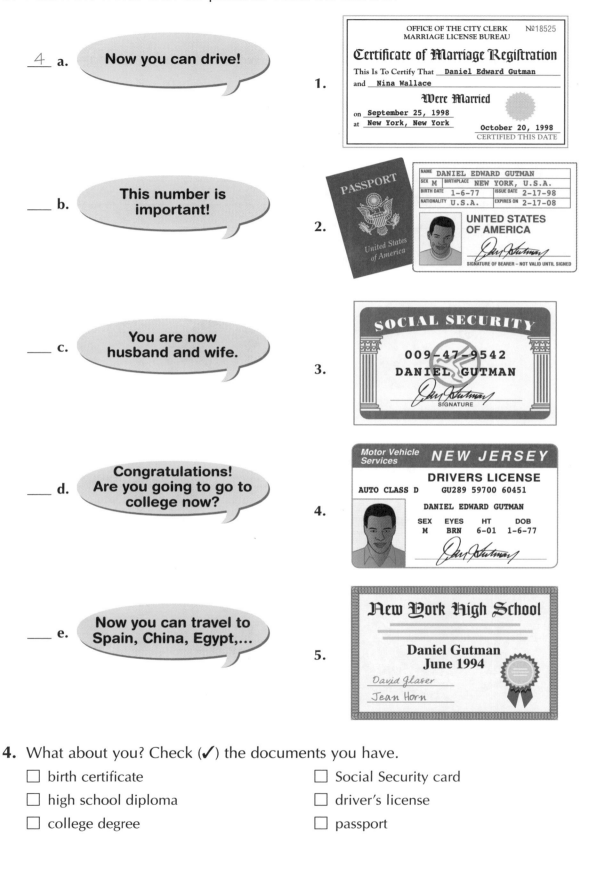

__4__ **a.** Now you can drive!

1. *[Certificate of Marriage Registration — OFFICE OF THE CITY CLERK, MARRIAGE LICENSE BUREAU №18525. This Is To Certify That Daniel Edward Gutman and Nina Wallace Were Married on September 25, 1998 at New York, New York. October 20, 1998 CERTIFIED THIS DATE]*

____ **b.** This number is important!

2. *[PASSPORT United States of America; NAME DANIEL EDWARD GUTMAN, SEX M, BIRTHPLACE NEW YORK, U.S.A., BIRTH DATE 1-6-77, ISSUE DATE 2-17-98, NATIONALITY U.S.A., EXPIRES ON 2-17-08, UNITED STATES OF AMERICA, SIGNATURE OF BEARER – NOT VALID UNTIL SIGNED]*

____ **c.** You are now husband and wife.

3. *[SOCIAL SECURITY 009-47-9542 DANIEL GUTMAN SIGNATURE]*

____ **d.** Congratulations! Are you going to go to college now?

4. *[Motor Vehicle Services NEW JERSEY DRIVERS LICENSE AUTO CLASS D GU289 59700 60451 DANIEL EDWARD GUTMAN, SEX M, EYES BRN, HT 6-01, DOB 1-6-77]*

____ **e.** Now you can travel to Spain, China, Egypt,...

5. *[New York High School, Daniel Gutman, June 1994, David Glaser, Jean Horn]*

4. What about you? Check (✓) the documents you have.

☐ birth certificate   ☐ Social Security card

☐ high school diploma   ☐ driver's license

☐ college degree   ☐ passport

Challenge   Look at **page 183** in this book. Complete the time line.

Feelings

1. Look in your dictionary. Write all the words that end in *-y* and *-ed*.

-Y	*-ED*	
thirsty	disgusted	_____
_____	_____	_____
_____	_____	_____
_____	_____	_____
_____	_____	
_____	_____	

2. How do these people feel? Use words from Exercise 1.

a. _____relieved_____   b. _____   c. _____

d. _____   e. _____

f. _____   g. _____   h. _____

i. _____   j. _____

3. Put these words in the correct columns.

bored	calm	comfortable	homesick	full	in love
in pain	nervous	proud	uncomfortable	sick	well

☺		☹	
calm		bored	

4. Complete the conversations. Use words from Exercise 3.

a. Are you hot? cold?   No. I'm <u>comfortable</u>, thanks.

b. So, do you like Sandy?   *Like?* I'm _____! ♥♥♥

c. What's wrong?   Oh, I'm _____. I miss my family, my friends, my country…

d. Wow! Your son got 100%!   Yes. I'm very _____ of him.

e. What's wrong?   I'm _____. Please call a doctor.

f. Is today your English test?   Yes. I'm very _____.

5. What about you? How do you feel when you…? Circle as many words as possible for each question. Add new words too.

a. **wake up**   sleepy   happy   calm   _____
b. **start a new class**   nervous   confused   excited   _____
c. **have problems in school** worried   upset   homesick   _____
d. **talk with your boss**   happy   nervous   comfortable   _____
e. _____   _____   _____   _____   _____

Challenge Look at **page 183** in this book. Answer the question.

A Graduation

1. Look in your dictionary. **True** or **False**?

a. A graduate is crying. _____False_____

b. The valedictorian is on the stage. _____

c. The guest speaker is wearing a cap and gown. _____

d. The photographer is taking a picture of the audience. _____

2. Match the photos with the captions. Write the letter.

a. b.

c. d.

e. f.

g. h.

_e_ 1. This is Mom crying.

____ 4. Miguel is giving his speech.

____ 2. Here's Dad taking a picture.

____ 5. Grandma is applauding.

____ 3. The podium

____ 6. The audience

____ 7. The proud graduates

____ 8. Miguel is getting his diploma.

3. Look at page 33 in your dictionary. Which invitation goes with the picture? Circle the letter.

a. b. c.

4. Look at the picture. Circle the correct words to complete the sentences.

a. This is a graduation <u>ceremony</u> / (party.)

b. Two guests are <u>hugging / kissing</u>.

c. There are four <u>guests / gifts</u> on the dance floor.

d. A <u>guest / caterer</u> is toasting the graduates.

e. A <u>DJ / caterer</u> is laughing.

f. There's a beautiful <u>banner / buffet</u> in the picture.

5. What about you? Circle all the things you like at parties.

a buffet   a DJ   gifts   a dance floor   Other: _____

Challenge Imagine you are having a graduation party. Design an invitation.

▶ **Go to page 171 for Another Look (Unit 2).**

Places to Live

1. Look in your dictionary. Where are they?

a. students   _college dormitory_

b. an elderly, physically-challenged woman   _____

c. a man with a newspaper   _____

2. Look at the chart. Circle the correct words to complete the statements.

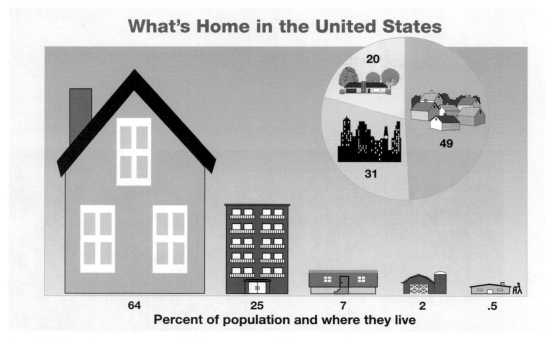

What's Home in the United States

20

49

31

64   25   7   2   .5

Percent of population and where they live

Compiled from 1994 U.S. Bureau of Census reports and the National Center for Health Statistics. (percents not exact)

a. Most people live in the city / (suburbs).

b. Only 20% of the people live in the suburbs / country.

c. About 31% live in the city / country.

d. Most people live in houses / apartment buildings.

e. About 7% of the people live in nursing homes / mobile homes.

f. Only 2% of the people live on farms / in apartment buildings.

3. What about you? Check (✓) the places where you've lived.

☐ city   ☐ suburbs   ☐ small town

☐ country   ☐ farm   ☐ ranch

☐ apartment building   ☐ house   ☐ mobile home

☐ college dormitory   ☐ townhouse   ☐ Other: _____

Challenge Take a class survey. Where do your classmates live? Write the results.

                 Example: *Five students live in apartments,...*

1. Look in your dictionary. Circle the correct words to complete the sentences.

    a. The woman in A wants to buy /(rent) an apartment.

    b. She talks to the manager / Realtor.

    c. The rent is $450 / $1,100.

    d. The man and woman in G are looking for a new apartment / house.

    e. The Realtor makes / man and woman make an offer.

    f. The rent / mortgage is $1,100.

2. Check (✔) the things you have to do to rent an apartment and/or buy a house.

	RENT AN APARTMENT	BUY A HOUSE
a. talk to the manager	✔	☐
b. make an offer	☐	☐
c. sign a lease	☐	☐
d. get a loan	☐	☐
e. take ownership	☐	☐
f. move in	☐	☐
g. pay the rent	☐	☐
h. pay the mortgage	☐	☐
i. unpack	☐	☐
j. arrange the furniture	☐	☐

3. What about you? Check (✔) the things you and your family have done in the last ten years.

    ☐ looked for a new apartment   ☐ made an offer

    ☐ looked for a new house   ☐ gotten a loan

    ☐ signed a rental agreement   ☐ paid a mortgage

    ☐ paid rent   ☐ talked to a manager

    ☐ talked to a Realtor   ☐ moved

Challenge How did you find your home? Write a paragraph.

Apartments

1. Look in your dictionary. Who said…?

a. **Good morning, Mrs. Cooper.**   _doorman_

b. **When can I get the keys to my apartment?**   _____

c. **Here's your lease. Please sign it here.**   _____

d. **There's a vacancy in Apartment 3.**   _____

e. **Hi, Jane. Thanks for getting my mail last week.**   _____

2. Look at the notice. **True** or **False**?

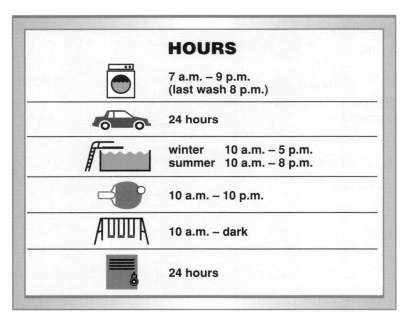

HOURS

🧺	7 a.m. – 9 p.m. (last wash 8 p.m.)
🚗	24 hours
🏊	winter 10 a.m. – 5 p.m. summer 10 a.m. – 8 p.m.
🏓	10 a.m. – 10 p.m.
🎢	10 a.m. – dark
🔒	24 hours

a. The swimming pool is always open until 8:00 P.M.   _False_

b. You can use the laundry room all night.   _____

c. The garage is always open.   _____

d. The playground always closes at 7:00 P.M.   _____

e. You can use the storage lockers at midnight.   _____

f. The rec room is open 24 hours.   _____

3. Circle the correct words to complete these notices.

a.
IN CASE OF FIRE, use the (fire exit) / peephole.

DO NOT use the elevator / stairs.

b.
NEW TENANTS: Please put your name on your balcony / mailbox.

c.
NOTICE
Do not throw...

Hangers   Aerosol cans

Glass bottles or jars   Newspapers

...down the trash chute / trash bin.

d.
ATTENTION ALL TENANTS: Do not allow strangers into the building. Always use the intercom / doorknob.

4. What about you? Does your home have a(n)...? Check (✓) **Yes** or **No**.

	YES	NO	IF YES, WHERE?
a. fire escape	☐	☐	_____
b. security system	☐	☐	_____
c. laundry room	☐	☐	_____
d. garage	☐	☐	_____
e. balcony	☐	☐	_____
f. air conditioner	☐	☐	_____
g. smoke detector	☐	☐	_____
h. lobby	☐	☐	_____
i. security gate	☐	☐	_____

Challenge Look at apartment ads in the newspaper. What do the apartments have? Use your dictionary for help. **Example:** *This apartment has an air conditioner...*

A House

1. Look in your dictionary. **Open** or **Closed**?

a. front door   <u>Closed</u>   d. mailbox   _____

b. shutters   _____   e. screen door   _____

c. storm door   _____   f. windows   _____

2. Look at this house. **True** or **False**?

a. This is a <u>two-story</u> house.   <u>False</u>

b. The house has a <u>gray</u> garage door.   _____

c. The doorbell is to the <u>right</u> of the front door.   _____

d. There is a chair on the <u>front walk</u>.   _____

e. The TV antenna is <u>in the front yard</u>.   _____

f. The chimney is <u>red</u>.   _____

g. The fence is <u>brown</u>.   _____

3. What about you? Would you like to live in this house? Check (✓) **Yes** or **No**.

☐ Yes   ☐ No   Why? _____

Challenge   Look at Exercise 2. Change the <u>underlined</u> words in the false sentences. Make the sentences true.

1. Look in your dictionary. Where's the…? Use the words in the box.

on the lawn	on the patio

a. garbage can   <u>on the patio</u>   **d.** furniture   _____

b. hammock   _____   **e.** sprinkler   _____

c. compost pile   _____   **f.** barbecue grill   _____

2. Put these words in the correct column.

~~bush~~   flower   flowerpot   garbage can   hedge   lawn
pruning shears   rake   shovel   trowel   watering can   wheelbarrow

GARDEN TOOLS   **VEGETATION**   **CONTAINERS**

              bush

_____   _____   _____

_____   _____   _____

_____   _____   _____

_____   _____   _____

3. Look at the garden and the list. Check (✓) the <u>completed</u> jobs.

Great Gardens
L A N D S C A P E R S

✓ water the plants

❑ weed the flower bed

❑ mow the lawn

❑ plant trees

❑ trim the hedge

❑ rake the leaves

Challenge   Look at the yard in your dictionary. What would you like to do there? Write a few sentences. Begin with *I'd like…*. **Example:** *I'd like to sit on the patio.*

A Kitchen

1. Look in your dictionary. Where can you find the...? Use the words in the box.

on	under

a. paper towels <u>under the cabinet</u>

b. dish drainer _____

c. bread _____

d. pot _____

e. broiler _____

f. garbage disposal _____

2. Look at the bar graph. Put the words in the correct column.

Based on information from: Shook, M. and R.: *It's About Time!* (NY: Penguin Books, 1992)

THINGS THAT LAST 10 YEARS		**THINGS THAT LAST 15 YEARS**
<u>blender</u>	_____	_____
_____	_____	_____
_____	_____	

3. What about you? Check (✓) the appliances you have. Answer the questions.

	WHERE IS IT?	**HOW LONG HAVE YOU HAD IT?**
☐ blender	_____	_____
☐ toaster oven	_____	_____
☐ coffeemaker	_____	_____
☐ mixer	_____	_____
☐ refrigerator	_____	_____
☐ microwave	_____	_____
☐ Other: _____	_____	_____

Challenge Look at the kitchen appliances in your dictionary. List the five you think are the most important. Compare your list with a classmate's list.

1. Look in your dictionary. **True** or **False**?

   a. The set of dishes is blue, white, and pink.   <u> True </u>

   b. There's a teapot on the tray.   <u>   </u>

   c. The ceiling fan has two light fixtures.   <u>   </u>

   d. The tablecloth is white.   <u>   </u>

   e. There's a vase in the china cabinet.   <u>   </u>

   f. The saltshaker is to the left of the pepper shaker.   <u>   </u>

   g. There's a mug on the dining room table.   <u>   </u>

2. Look at this table setting. Complete the sentences.

   a. The <u> plate </u> is white.

   b. It's on the purple _____.

   c. The green _____ is on the _____.

   d. There are two _____ to the left of the plate.

   e. They aren't on the pink _____. They're next to it.

   f. There are two _____. They're to the right of the plate.

   g. There's also a _____ to the right of the plate.

   h. There's a _____. It's for water.

3. What about you? How does your table setting look? Draw a picture on your own paper. Then complete the chart.

ITEM	HOW MANY?	WHERE?
knife		
fork		
spoon		
plate		
bowl		

ITEM	HOW MANY?	WHERE?
glass		
place mat		
napkin		
Other: _____		
_____		

Challenge   Tell a classmate how to draw the place setting from your table. Does it look the same as your picture in Exercise 3?

A Living Room

1. Look in your dictionary. How many ... are there?

   a. throw pillows ___3___   **b.** logs _____   **c.** baskets _____

   d. paintings _____   **e.** lightbulbs in the track lighting _____

2. Look at the Millers' new living room. Cross out the items they have <u>already</u> bought.

TO BUY

~~couch~~   carpet
love seat   track lighting
armchair   floor lamp
color TV   plant
stereo   magazine holder
wall unit   drapes
bookcase   fire screen
coffee table   logs
throw pillows end table

3. What about you? Look at the checklist in Exercise 2. List the items you have. Use your own paper.

_____ **Challenge**   Write six sentences about the Millers' living room. **Example:** *They have a couch, but they don't have a love seat.*

1. Look in your dictionary. Where are they? Check (✔) the correct columns.

	SINK	BATHTUB/SHOWER	WALL	FLOOR
a. towel racks		✔	✔	
b. hot water				
c. faucets				
d. tiles				
e. mats				
f. drains				
g. toothbrush holder				

2. Look at the ad. Circle the correct words to complete the sentences.

a. The (bath mat)/ rubber mat is $9.99.
b. The hamper / wastebasket is $6.99.
c. The bath towel / hand towel is $5.99.
d. The soap dish / soap is $2.99.
e. The toilet brush / toothbrush is $4.99.
f. The toilet paper / washcloth is $3.99.
g. The towel rack / scale is $27.99.

Challenge Look at an ad or in a store. What do these items cost?

a toothbrush _____

a soap dish _____

a wastebasket _____

a bath mat _____

A Bedroom

1. Look in your dictionary. What color is the...?

    a. bedspread __purple__   **b.** mattress _____   **c.** lamp _____

2. Cross out the word that doesn't belong.

a. They're electric.	~~mirror~~	outlet	light switch	clock radio
b. They're soft.	pillowcase	dust ruffle	headboard	blanket
c. They're part of a bed.	mattress	lamp	box spring	bed frame
d. They're on the floor.	bed frame	lampshade	rug	night table
e. They make the room dark.	lampshade	curtains	window shade	dresser
f. You put things in them.	closet	drawer	photographs	night table

3. Complete the conversations. Use words from Exercise 2.

    a. Lee: What time is it?

        Mom: I don't know. There's a __clock radio__
                on the night table.

    b. Tom: I'm cold.

        Ana: Here's an extra _____ .

    c. Ray: The bed's uncomfortable.

        Mia: The _____ is too soft.

    d. Amir: There's no window shade.

        Marwa: Close the _____ .

    e. Bill: My sweater's not in the drawer.

        Molly: Look in the _____ .

4. What about you? Check (✔) the items that are on your bed.

☐ fitted sheet   Color: _____

☐ flat sheet   Color: _____

☐ bedspread   Color: _____

☐ pillow(s)   How many? _____   Hard or soft? _____

☐ mattress   Hard or soft? _____

☐ blankets   How many? _____

☐ Other: _____

Challenge   Write a paragraph describing your bedroom.

1. Look in your dictionary. Which four items are for safety?

a. _____night-light_____   c. _____

b. _____   d. _____

2. Look at Sue and Mindy's room. There are 12 dolls in the room. Find and circle them.

Write the locations of the dolls. Use your own paper. Use *on, under,* and *in.*

Example: *under the bunk bed*

3. What about you? Check (✔) the things you played with when you were a child.

☐ dolls   ☐ teddy bears   ☐ crayons   ☐ puzzles

☐ stuffed animals ☐ balls   ☐ Other: _____

Challenge Look at the toys you checked in Exercise 3. Write a paragraph about your favorite one.

Housework

1. Look in your dictionary. What are the people doing? Use the *-ing* form of the verb.

a. (**Can we do this with magazines, too?**)   <u>recycling the newspapers</u>

b. (**Dad, does this teddy bear go here?**)   _____

c. (**I like this new bedspread.**)   _____

d. (**Is this the last plate, Dad?**)   _____

2. Look at the room. What housework did Todd do? Check (✓) the <u>completed</u> jobs.

To Do
☑ wash the sheets
☐ change the sheets
☐ sweep the floor
☐ empty the wastebasket
☐ dust the dresser
☐ clean the sink
☐ mop the bathroom floor
☐ take out the newspapers

3. What about you? How often do you…? Check (✓) the correct column.

	ALWAYS	SOMETIMES	NEVER
dust the furniture			
polish the furniture			
recycle the newspapers			
wash the dishes			
vacuum the carpet			
wipe the counter			
scrub the floor			
put away clothes			
Other: _____			

Challenge Write a *To Do* list of housework for this week.

1. Look in your dictionary. What can you use to clean the…?

WINDOWS   **FLOOR**   **DISHES**

glass cleaner   _____   _____   _____

_____   _____   _____   _____

                                  _____   _____

2. Match each item with the correct coupon. Write the letter.

To Buy:

_d_ 1. feather duster

____ 2. steel-wool pads

____ 3. sponges

____ 4. pail

____ 5. cleanser

____ 6. trash bags

____ 7. dishwashing liquid

____ 8. rubber gloves

____ 9. vacuum cleaner bags

3. What about you? Look at the cleaning supplies in Exercise 2. Which ones do you have? What do you use them for? Make a list on your own paper.

Example: _feather duster—dust the desk_

Challenge   Look in a store or at newspaper ads. Write the prices of some cleaning supplies that you use.

Household Problems and Repairs

1. Look in your dictionary. Who said…?

a. (I'm up on the roof.) _roofer_

b. (Good-bye termites!) _____

c. (I'm turning the power on again.) _____

d. (I'll fix the toilet next.) _____

e. (I'm fixing the lock on the front door.) _____

f. (I have one more step to do.) _____

g. (I'm putting in new windows.) _____

2. Look at John's bathroom. There are seven problems. Find and circle them.

True or **False**? Change the <u>underlined</u> words in the false sentences. Make the sentences true.

a. The <u>sink</u> faucet is dripping. _False. The bathtub faucet is dripping._

b. The <u>window</u> is broken. _____

c. There are <u>ants</u> near the sink. _____

d. The <u>light</u> isn't working. _____

e. The <u>sink</u> is overflowing. _____

f. The <u>mirror</u> is cracked. _____

3. Look at the picture in Exercise 2 and these ads. Who should John call? Complete his list. Include the company name, the phone number, and the problem(s). (*Hint:* John will use some of the companies for more than one problem.)

224 YELLOW PAGES

ABC ELECTRIC CORP.
• Licensed Electricians
• Free Estimates
555-2656

Free estimates
HAMPTON CARPENTERS INC.
• closets • wall units
• shelves • shutters
• cabinets • bookcases
555-7367

JACK O. TRADES
GENERAL REPAIRS
No job is too small.
555-8356

Keys Made While-U-Wait
UNIVERSITY LOCKSMITHS
Your one-stop security shop
555-9946

EXTERMINALL PEST CONTROL
Fast and Safe
Residential and Commercial
555-4789

Affordable Home Remodeling
HARMON ROOFING REPAIRS
• All types of roofing
• leaders & gutters
• Licensed & Insured
555-7587
"We care about yo

Tell the Advertisers you found them in the **Yellow Pages**

EMERGENCY SERVICES
24 HOURS
7 DAYS A WEEK
Free Flow Plumbing Co.
555-2233

Let your fing
the walking i
Yellow Pa

Why wonder
buy it?
The **Yellow**
tell you *wher*

Call

1. exterminator   555-4789
   a. cockroaches
2. _____ _____
   a. dripping faucet
   b. _____
   c. _____
3. _____ _____
   a. _____
4. _____ _____
   a. _____
   b. _____

Challenge Look at the problems in Exercise 3. Who fixes them in <u>your</u> home? Make a list. Use the phone book if necessary. **Example:** *broken window—my cousin Paul*

▶ **Go to page 172 for Another Look (Unit 3).**

49

Fruit

1. Look in your dictionary. Write the name of the fruit.
   a. They're to the left of the pears.   _peaches_
   b. They're below the apricots.   _____
   c. They're above the nuts.   _____
   d. They're to the right of the cantaloupes.   _____ and _____
   e. They're to the right of the raspberries and blueberries. _____
   f. One of them is rotten.   _____

2. Complete the ad. Use the words in the box.

apples	avocadoes	grapefruit	grapes	lemons	limes
	oranges	pears	~~pineapples~~	strawberries	

3. What about you? Look at the fruits in Exercise 2. Make a shopping list. Use your own paper. What will you buy? How much or how many? How much will it cost?

   Example: *2 avocadoes—$1.98*

   Challenge Make a list of fruit from your country.

1. Look in your dictionary. Which vegetables are…? Put them in the correct column.

YELLOW/ORANGE	GREEN		RED
carrots			

2. Look at the chart.

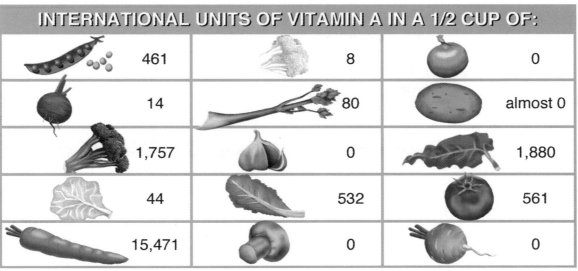

INTERNATIONAL UNITS OF VITAMIN A IN A 1/2 CUP OF:

	461		8		0
	14		80		almost 0
	1,757		0		1,880
	44		532		561
	15,471		0		0

Based on information from: Netzer, C.: *The Encyclopedia of Food Values.* (NY: Dell Publishing, 1992)

Which has more vitamin A? Circle the correct answer.

a. lettuce / spinach

b. broccoli / cauliflower

c. beets / turnips

d. carrots / celery

e. potatoes / tomatoes

f. cabbage / lettuce

3. What about you? How often do you eat these vegetables? Circle the numbers.

CARROTS	0	1	2	3	4	4+	TIMES A WEEK
BROCCOLI	0	1	2	3	4	4+	TIMES A WEEK
SPINACH	0	1	2	3	4	4+	TIMES A WEEK
TOMATOES	0	1	2	3	4	4+	TIMES A WEEK

Challenge Make a list of vegetables from your country.

Meat and Poultry

1. Look in your dictionary. Which meats have bones? Which meats don't have bones? Make a list on your own paper.

   Example: *with bones—steak*   *boneless—roast beef*

2. Look at the chart. Write the cooking times. Use numbers.

	SIZE	COOKING TIME	METHOD
	1½" thick	10 min.*	broiler
	½" thick	3 min.*	broiler
	5–8 lbs.	30 min./lb.	oven
	8–20 lbs.	20 min./lb.	oven
	8–12 lbs.	3–4 hrs.	oven
	2½–3 lbs.	1¼ hrs.	oven

*each side

   a. 10 lb. turkey   <u>3–4 hours</u>   d. 6 lb. leg of lamb _____

   b. 10 lb. ham   _____   e. 1½" thick steak _____

   c. ½" thick piece   _____   f. 3 lb. chicken _____
       of liver

3. Label the chicken parts. Use the words in the box.

~~breast~~   drumstick   thigh   wing

   a. <u>breast</u>   c. _____

   b. _____   d. _____

4. What about you? Check (✓) the meat and poultry you eat.

   ☐ veal cutlets   ☐ bacon   ☐ duck   ☐ gizzards   ☐ tripe

   Challenge Take a survey. Ask five people which meats and poultry they eat.

1. Look in your dictionary. Write the names of the seafood.

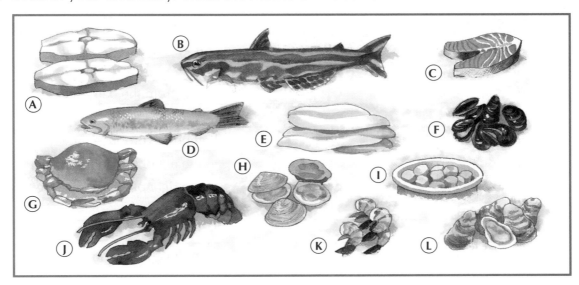

a. ___halibut___   d. _____   g. _____   j. _____

b. _____   e. _____   h. _____   k. _____

c. _____   f. _____   i. _____   l. _____

2. Look at the sandwich and the order form. Check (✔) the correct boxes.

Sandwich Order

Meat/Fish	**Cheese**
☑ smoked turkey	☐ American
☐ roast beef	☐ jack
☐ corned beef	☐ Swiss
☐ salami	☐ cheddar
☐ pastrami	
☐ filet of sole	

Bread	**Side**
☐ white	☐ potato salad
☐ wheat	☐ pasta salad
☐ rye	☐ coleslaw

3. What about you? Complete your order with the food from the form in Exercise 2.

A _____ sandwich on _____ bread with a side

of _____ .

Challenge Ask five classmates what they want from the deli. Write their orders.

The Market

1. Look at the market in your dictionary. Where are these items? Complete the chart.

	SECTION NAME	LOCATION
a. soup	canned goods	aisle 1B
b. chicken		
c. tomatoes		across from the dairy section
d. bread		
e. milk		behind the produce section
f. soda		to the left of the doors
g. ice cream		to the right of the produce section
h. flour		
i. toilet paper		
j. candy bars		near the checkstand

2. Complete the conversations. Use the words in the box.

> **Bagger**   **bottle return**   **cart**   **Checker**
> **checkstands**   ~~**Manager**~~   **plastic**

Amy: Excuse me. Where do I take these empty soda bottles?

   Manager : To the _____. Near aisle 1.
      a.   **b.**

Amy: I'll get a shopping basket.

Jason: Get a shopping _____! We have a lot on our list.
                   c.

Amy: Look at the _____!
                 d.

Jason: Oh, no. The lines are really long.

Jason: What's the total?

_____: $87.67
  e.

Amy: Can we have four bags?

_____: Sure. Paper or _____?
  f.   **g.**

3. Look at Amy and Jason's shopping list. Put the items in the correct category.

To Buy

tuna   butter
eggs   flour
bread   sugar
aluminum foil milk
lemon cake   oil
rolls   bottled water
yogurt   plastic wrap
ice cream   soda
potato chips cheddar cheese
beans   gum

CANNED GOODS	FROZEN FOODS	BAKING PRODUCTS	DAIRY SECTION
tuna			

BEVERAGES	PAPER PRODUCTS	BAKED GOODS	SNACK FOODS

4. Look at the things Amy and Jason bought. Cross the items off the shopping list in Exercise 3.

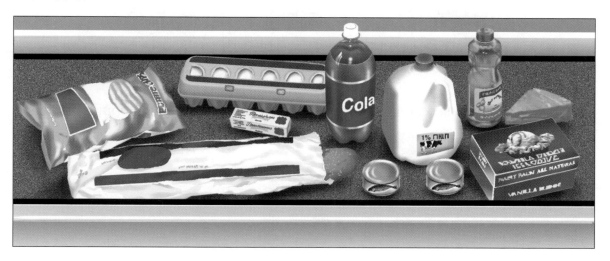

Challenge Make a shopping list. Write the section for each item. **Example:** *scallops—fish section*

Containers and Packaged Foods

1. Look at **pages 54 and 55** in your dictionary. Write the container or package for these items.

   a. beans   <u> can </u>   **c.** instant coffee   <u>   </u>

   b. cake mix   <u>   </u>   **d.** margarine   <u>   </u>

2. Complete these coupons. Use the words in the box.

bag	bottle	carton	loaf
six-pack	package	roll	~~tube~~

3. Tiffany used all the coupons in Exercise 2. Write her shopping list. Use your own paper.

   Example: *2 tubes of toothpaste*

Challenge   Which foods do you <u>think</u> are in your refrigerator? Make a list. Then check your answers at home. Include the foods and their containers. **Example:** *a bottle of soda*

56

1. Look in your dictionary. Match the abbreviations with the words. Write the number.

<u>3</u> **a.** oz.   **1.** teaspoon

___ **b.** lb.   **2.** gallon

___ **c.** pt.   **3.** ounce

___ **d.** qt.   **4.** pound

___ **e.** c.   **5.** quart

___ **f.** tsp.   **6.** cup

___ **g.** TBS.   **7.** tablespoon

___ **h.** gal.   **8.** pint

2. Write the weight or measurement. Use the complete word, not the abbreviation.

a. <u>1¹/2 pounds of potatoes</u>   **b.** _____

c. _____   **d.** _____

e. _____   **f.** _____

<u>**Challenge**</u> Look at **page 183** in this book. Follow the instructions.

Food Preparation

1. Look in your dictionary. Read the recipe. <u>Underline</u> all the food preparation words.

> **Baked Carrots**
>
> 1 lb.(450 g.) carrots   1 tsp. sugar
> 3 TBS. butter   1/2 cup water
> 1 small onion
> salt, pepper, nutmeg
>
> <u>Chop</u> the onion. Peel and grate the
> carrots. Grease a small pan.

> (continued)
> Add the onion and cook until soft. Stir
> in the carrots. Add the sugar, salt,
> pepper, nutmeg, and water. Pour into a
> covered casserole dish. Bake at
> 350°F(180°C) until soft, about 30–40
> minutes.

2. Look at the recipe in Exercise 1. Number the pictures in order.

___ a.   ___ b.   _1_ c.   ___ d.

___ e.   ___ f.   ___ g.   ___ h.

3. Look at the pictures. Circle the correct words to complete the recipe.

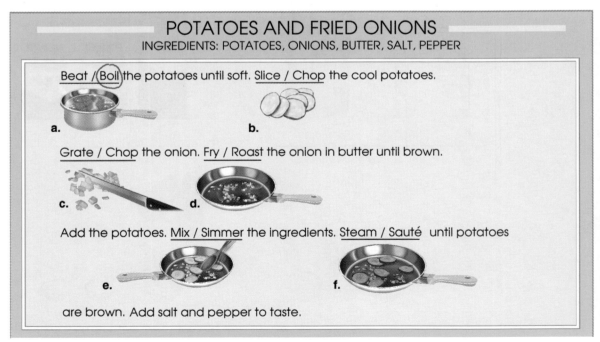

POTATOES AND FRIED ONIONS
INGREDIENTS: POTATOES, ONIONS, BUTTER, SALT, PEPPER

Beat / (Boil) the potatoes until soft. <u>Slice / Chop</u> the cool potatoes.

a.   b.

<u>Grate / Chop</u> the onion. <u>Fry / Roast</u> the onion in butter until brown.

c.   d.

Add the potatoes. <u>Mix / Simmer</u> the ingredients. <u>Steam / Sauté</u> until potatoes

e.   f.

are brown. Add salt and pepper to taste.

Challenge   Write the recipe for one of your favorite foods. Share it with a classmate.

58

1. Look in your dictionary. **True** or **False**?

   a. The grater is below the steamer.   _____False_____

   b. There's lettuce in the colander.   _____

   c. The whisk and strainer are on the wall.   _____

   d. The ladle is in the pot.   _____

   e. The lid is on the double boiler.   _____

   f. The spatula is above the tongs.   _____

2. Match the words that go together. Write the number.

   _6_ **a.** cake   **1.** beater

   ___ **b.** mixing   **2.** opener

   ___ **c.** egg   **3.** boiler

   ___ **d.** garlic   **4.** sheet

   ___ **e.** double   **5.** holder

   ___ **f.** pot   **6.** pan

   ___ **g.** rolling   **7.** bowl

   ___ **h.** cookie   **8.** press

   ___ **i.** can   **9.** pin

3. Fill in the blanks. Use the words in Exercise 2.

SOME KITCHEN UTENSILS

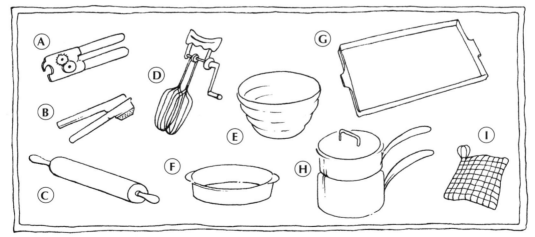

   a. _can opener_   **d.** _____   **g.** _____

   b. _____   **e.** _____   **h.** _____

   c. _____   **f.** _____   **i.** _____

Challenge List the five most important kitchen utensils. Why are they important?

            Example: *pot—to cook spaghetti, soups, and vegetables*

Fast Food

1. Look in your dictionary. What can you eat or drink with…?

    A STRAW

    soda

    YOUR FINGERS

2. Check (✓) the items that are on the hamburger.

    Hamburger with:

    ☑ cheese ☐ ketchup
    ☐ onions ☐ mustard
    ☐ lettuce ☐ mayonnaise
    ☐ tomato ☐ relish

3. Look at the information. Number the items in order of their calories. (Number 1 has the most calories.)

16 cal.	15 cal.	101 cal.	15 cal.	46 cal.

    ___ sugar   _1_ mayonnaise   ___ mustard/relish   ___ ketchup

4. What about you? Check (✓) the condiments you use. What foods do you put them on?

    CONDIMENT   **FOODS**

    ☐ ketchup   _____

    ☐ mustard   _____

    ☐ mayonnaise _____

    ☐ relish   _____

Challenge Find out how many calories are in some of your favorite fast foods.

1. Look in your dictionary. Complete the orders.

a. Scrambled eggs, _____sausage_____, and _____.

b. A _____ on whole wheat bread.

c. _____, _____, and corn.

d. _____ and bacon.

e. Steak, a _____, and vegetables.

f. Pasta and _____.

g. Apple _____.

2. Look at the food. Complete the order.

FOOD ORDER

TABLE

roast chicken

TOTAL

GRATUITIES NOT INCLUDED

3. What about you? What's your favorite…?

soup _____ dessert _____ hot beverage _____

_____ **Challenge** Show five people the coffee shop menu in your dictionary. Write their orders.

A Restaurant

1. Look in your dictionary. Who…?

   a. washes dishes   _dishwasher_

   b. leaves a tip   _____

   c. takes orders   _____

   d. cooks food   _____

   e. carries dessert trays   _____

   f. seats customers   _____

2. Look at the order and the place setting.

onion soup
house salad
steak
broccoli
mashed potatoes
garlic bread
half bottle of
   red wine
coffee

Check (✓) the items the place setting still needs.

☐ dinner plate	☐ wine glass	☐ dinner fork
☑ salad plate	☐ cup	☐ steak knife
☐ soup bowl	☐ saucer	☐ knife
☐ bread-and-butter plate	☐ napkin	☐ teaspoon
☐ water glass	☐ salad fork	☐ soupspoon

3. Look at the menu. Complete the check.

Menu

Soup of the day $3.50
House salad 2.50

Fish of the day 15.50
Chicken l'orange 10.50
Sirloin steak 17.50

Vegetables 1.50
Potatoes 1.50

Cherry pie 3.50
with ice cream 4.00
Coconut cake 3.50

Coffee or tea 1.50

```
             The Bistro
           242 WEST STREET
              555-0700
            GUEST CHECK
black bean soup              $3.50
house salad              _____
grilled salmon           _____
peas                     _____
french fries             _____
cherry pie w.vanilla ice cream _____
coffee                   _____

Subtotal                 _____
Tax (5%)                   $1.50
Total                    _____
             Thank you!
       Hope to see you again soon
```

4. In the United States, most restaurant patrons leave a tip. The tip is usually 15% of the subtotal. Look at the check in Exercise 3. Complete the sentences with the correct answers.

a. The subtotal is ___$30.00___ . $30.00 $31.50 $36.22

b. A 15% tip is _____ . $1.50 $4.50 $4.72

c. You should leave this tip on the _____ .   menu   table   dessert tray

5. What about you? Do people leave tips for the server in your country? _____ .
If yes, how much? _____ Where do they leave it? _____

Challenge   Look at the menu in Exercise 3. Order a meal. Figure out the subtotal, 5% tax, the total, and a 15% tip.

▶ Go to page 173 for Another Look (Unit 4).

Clothing I

1. Look in your dictionary. What color is/are the…?

    a. jumpsuit   _orange_   **d.** overalls   _____

    b. jeans   _____   **e.** sweatpants   _____

    c. cardigan sweater _____   **f.** jumper   _____

2. Which clothes do women usually wear? Men? Both women and men? Put the words from the box in the correct space.

~~blouse~~   dress   evening gown   jeans   jumper   leggings maternity dress   pants   skirt   sports coat   sports shirt   suit   sweater three-piece suit   tunic   T-shirt   turtleneck   tuxedo   uniform   vest

Women Only

blouse

_____

_____

_____

_____

_____

_____

Women and Men

_____

_____

_____

_____

_____

_____

_____

Men Only

_____

_____

_____

_____

3. Put the names of the clothing items on the list. Write the color, too.

To Pack for Chicago

a. _blue jeans_ and _white T-shirt_

b._____

c._____

d._____

e._____ and _____

4. Match the activity with the clothes from Exercise 3. Write the letter.

The Parkview Hotel 🏨

Saturday

_e_ 1. Meet Jane in exercise room — 7:30 A.M.

___ 2. Meeting in Conference Room 23 — 9:00 A.M.–3:00 P.M.

___ 3. Relax in hotel room — 3:00 P.M.–5:30 P.M.

___ 4. Dinner at The Grille with Greg Haines — 6:30 P.M.

___ 5. Dance party at the Grand Hotel Ballroom — 9:00 P.M.

5. What about you? When do you wear these clothes? Check (✔) the correct columns.

	AT SCHOOL	AT WORK	AT HOME	AT A PARTY	NEVER
suit					
jeans					
shorts					
sweatshirt and pants					
tuxedo or gown					
uniform					
Other: _____					

Challenge Look at the clothes in your dictionary. List eight items you have. When do you wear them?
Example: dress—I wear it at work.

Clothing II

1. Look in your dictionary. **True** or **False**?

   a. The man with the gray cap is wearing a jacket. _____True_____

   b. The woman with the ski cap is wearing green tights. _____

   c. The woman in the poncho is wearing yellow rainboots. _____

   d. The man with the baseball cap is wearing sunglasses. _____

2. Circle the correct words to complete the ad.

Dress for the Snow

Jessica is wearing a dark blue <u>down vest</u> /(parka,)
a.
red <u>ski cap / ski mask</u>, and green <u>gloves / mittens</u>.
b.   **c.**
Justin is wearing a black leather <u>coat / jacket</u>, purple
d.
<u>earmuffs / hat</u>, and a red <u>scarf / poncho</u>.
e.   **f.**

Dress for the Sun

Kimberly is wearing a <u>baseball cap / straw hat</u>,
g.
pink <u>swimming trunks / swimsuit</u>, and
h.
a white <u>cover-up / windbreaker</u>. Her
i.
<u>raincoat / umbrella</u> and <u>cap / sunglasses</u>
j.   **k.**
protect her from the sun.

3. What about you? Circle the correct words to complete the statements.

   a. I <u>am / am not</u> wearing a jacket or coat today.

   b. I <u>wear / don't wear</u> sunglasses.

   c. I <u>sometimes / never</u> wear a hat.

Challenge Find pictures of people in a newspaper, magazine, or your dictionary. Describe their clothes. **Example:** *She's wearing a dark blue skirt, a white pullover,…*

1. Look in your dictionary. What color is/are the...?

a. bike shorts   <u>black</u>   **e.** leotard   _____

b. slippers   _____   **f.** nightgown   _____

c. half slip   _____   **g.** kneesocks   _____

d. long underwear   _____   **h.** bathrobe   _____

2. Look at the ad. Complete the bill.

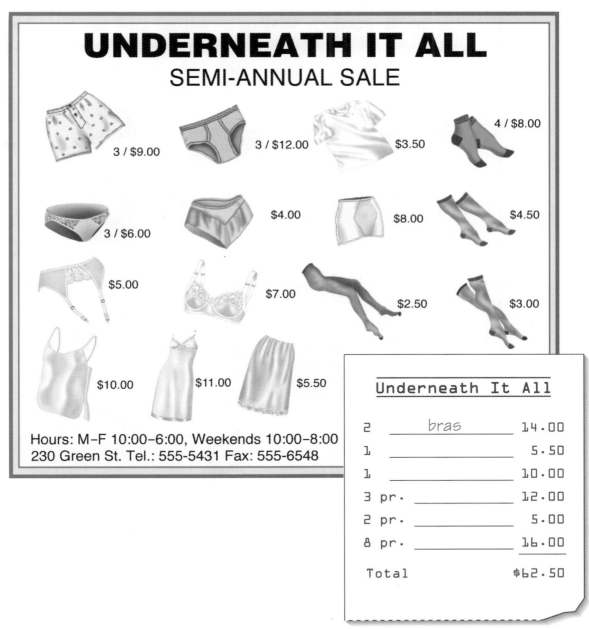

Challenge   Choose clothes from the ad in Exercise 2. Write a bill. Figure out the total.

1. Look in your dictionary. How many ... can you see?

a. salesclerks _____2_____   d. bow ties in the case _____

b. people in line _____   e. handbags on the case _____

c. hats in the case _____   f. scarves _____

2. Put the words from the box in alphabetical order to complete the store directory. Then look at the accessories. Write the correct display case number for each item.

purses	hats	necklaces	scarves	earrings	key chains
ties	handkerchiefs	belts	rings	wallets	pins	~~backpacks~~
	chains	watches	bracelets	

STORE DIRECTORY

	Display case
backpacks	3
_____	6
_____	1
_____	2
_____	1
_____	9
_____	10
_____	7
_____	2
_____	4
_____	3
_____	4
_____	9
_____	5
_____	7
_____	8

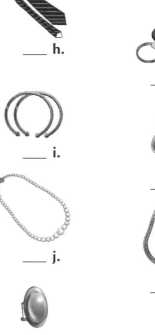

__7__ a.

_____ b.

_____ c.

_____ d.

_____ e.

_____ f.

_____ g.

_____ h.

_____ i.

_____ j.

_____ k.

_____ l.

_____ m.

_____ n.

_____ o.

_____ p.

3. Cross out the word that doesn't belong.

    a. Things you wear around your neck   tie   ~~belt~~   scarf   locket

    b. Types of necklaces   beads   bracelet   chain   pearls

    c. Things you can keep a change purse in   backpack   shoulder bag   wallet   tote bag

    d. Types of shoes   sandals   boots   pumps   suspenders

    e. Parts of a shoe   sole   pin   heel   toe

4. Complete the ad. Use the words in the box.

> athletic shoes   ~~boots~~   high heels   hiking boots
>
> loafers   oxfords   sandals   tennis shoes

The Good Sole SALE
Save 20% on men's and women's shoes

a. _boots_   b. _____   c. _____   d. _____

e. _____   f. _____   g. _____   h. _____

Located at the Lincoln Mall. Route 65.

5. What about you? Check (✔) the items you have.

    ☐ chain   ☐ watch   ☐ pierced earrings

    ☐ clip-on earrings   ☐ belt buckle   ☐ key chain

Challenge   List the kinds of shoes you have. When do you wear them? **Example:** *boots—I wear them in cold or wet weather.*

Describing Clothes

1. Look at the yellow sweaters in your dictionary. **True** or **False**?

   a. They are new. _____True_____
   b. They have a V-neck. _____
   c. They come in four sizes. _____

   d. They are long-sleeved. _____
   e. They have stains. _____
   f. They are checked. _____

2. Match the opposites. Write the number.

   _4_ **a.** new
   ___ **b.** short
   ___ **c.** formal
   ___ **d.** fancy
   ___ **e.** heavy
   ___ **f.** loose
   ___ **g.** narrow
   ___ **h.** high

   1. plain
   2. wide
   3. tight
   4. old
   5. low
   6. casual
   7. light
   8. long

3. Look at the pictures. Describe the problems. Use words from Exercise 2 and the word *too*.

   a. They're _too short_.   **b.** They're _____.   **c.** They're _____.

   d. It's _____.   **e.** It's _____.

4. Look at the order form. Circle the correct words to complete the statements.

Item #	Page #	Description	Size	Color	Quantity	Item Price	Total
		CLOTHES TOWN CATALOG STORE			ORDER TOLL-FREE 1-800-555-4627		
563218	3	wool sweater	S	red and black striped	1	#15.00	#15.00
0421578	7	silk T-shirt	XS	light blue	1	17.00	17.00
962143	12	linen jacket	M	black	1	62.00	62.00
583614	8	rayon shirt	L	paisley	1	18.00	18.00
216983	10	loose-fit jeans	7	black	2	25.00	50.00

a. The customer wants a <u>medium</u> / (<u>small</u>) sweater.

b. The customer wants a <u>long</u> / <u>large</u> paisley shirt.

c. The paisley shirt is <u>cotton</u> / <u>synthetic</u>.

d. The T-shirt is <u>solid</u> / <u>polka-dotted</u>.

e. The material of the jacket is <u>heavy</u> / <u>light</u>.

f. The jeans are <u>baggy</u> / <u>tight</u>.

5. What about you? Look at the ad. Choose two items to order. Add them to the order form in Exercise 4.

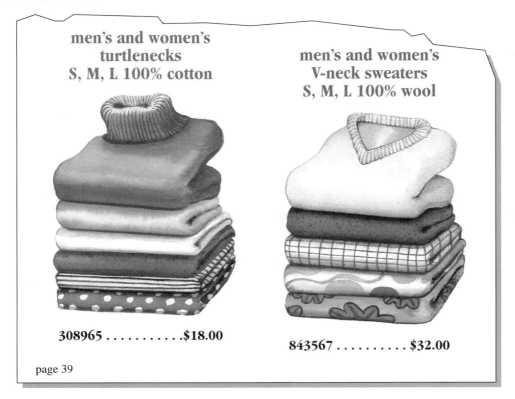

men's and women's
turtlenecks
S, M, L 100% cotton

men's and women's
V-neck sweaters
S, M, L 100% wool

308965 . . . .$18.00

843567 . . . . $32.00

page 39

Challenge Describe the clothes you are wearing today. Include the color and material.

Doing the Laundry

1. Look in your dictionary. Where is the...? Use *on* in your answer.

a. bleach _____on the shelf_____   c. spray starch _____

b. fabric softener _____   d. pair of socks _____

2. Match the pictures with the instructions. Write the number.

_5_ **a.**

b.

c.

d.

e.

f.

g.

1. **Clean the lint trap!**

2. **Iron the shirt!**

3. **Fold the clothes!**

4. **Unload the washer!**

5. **Sort the clothes!**

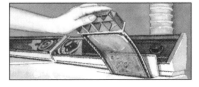
6. **Load the washer!**

7. **Wash the shirt!**

Challenge Think of five clothing items. How do you clean them? **Example:** *my jeans—I put them in the washer. Then I dry them on the clothesline.*

1. Look in your dictionary. Who said…?

a.  **Please let out the waistband, too.**   _customer_

b. **I love this new sewing machine.**   _____

c. **I'm almost finished with this hemline.**   _____

2. Look at the pictures. Check (✔) the alterations the tailor made.

Altered States

- ☑ sew on buttons
- ☐ repair zipper
- ☐ lengthen hemline
- ☐ shorten hemline
- ☐ take in waistband
- ☐ let out waistband
- ☐ repair pocket
- ☐ repair seam

Before   **After**

3. List the items in the sewing basket. Include the number.

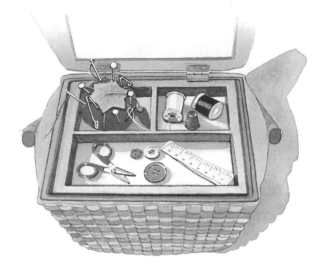

1 tape measure
_____
_____
_____
_____
_____
_____
_____
_____
_____

Challenge Write about some clothing alterations. **Example:** *My jeans were too long. My cousin shortened them.*

▶ **Go to page 174 for Another Look (Unit 5).**

1. Look in your dictionary. Cross out the word that doesn't belong.

a. **Face**	nose	jaw	chin	~~neck~~
b. **Inside the body**	liver	intestines	abdomen	stomach
c. **The foot**	knee	heel	ankle	toe
d. **The skeleton**	pelvis	rib cage	skull	brain
e. **The hand**	finger	toenail	palm	wrist
f. **The senses**	taste	see	ear	smell

2. Label the parts of the face. Use the words in the box.

ear	eye	eyebrow	eyelashes	eyelid	cheek	chin
forehead	gums	~~hair~~	jaw	lip	mouth	nose	teeth

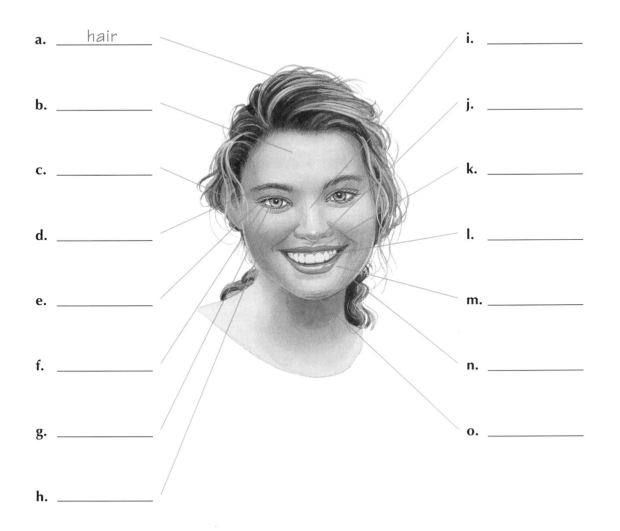

a. _____hair_____

b. _____

c. _____

d. _____

e. _____

f. _____

g. _____

h. _____

i. _____

j. _____

k. _____

l. _____

m. _____

n. _____

o. _____

3. Look at the picture. Check (✔) the parts of the body that are NOT covered by clothes.

- ✔ arms
- ☐ back
- ☐ calves
- ☐ chest
- ☐ elbows
- ☐ fingers
- ☐ feet
- ☐ hands
- ☐ head
- ☐ knees
- ☐ legs
- ☐ neck
- ☐ shoulders
- ☐ waist

4. Look at the picture. Match the words with the parts of the body. Write the number.

- _4_ **a.** heart
- ___ **b.** kidney
- ___ **c.** lung
- ___ **d.** liver
- ___ **e.** gallbladder
- ___ **f.** bladder
- ___ **g.** throat
- ___ **h.** stomach
- ___ **i.** pancreas
- ___ **j.** brain
- ___ **k.** intestines

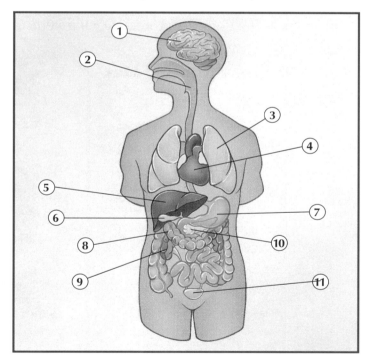

5. What about you? <u>Underline</u> the parts of the body that are NOT OK for men to show on the street in your country. Circle the parts of the body that are NOT OK for women.

arms	abdomen	elbows	face	hair	mouth
shoulders	back	chest	knees	calves	feet

Challenge   Choose five parts of the body. What are their functions? **Example:** *brain—We use it to think.*

Personal Hygiene

1. Look in your dictionary. Cross out the word that doesn't belong.

a.	shower cap	soap	~~hair spray~~	talcum powder
b.	electric shaver	razor blade	aftershave	sunscreen
c.	hair clip	emery board	polish	polish remover
d.	barrettes	eyebrow pencil	clips	hair gel
e.	blush	foundation	eyeliner	deodorant
f.	moisturizer	shampoo	blow dryer	conditioner
g.	toothbrush	comb	dental floss	toothpaste

2. Look at Exercise 1. Write the letter of the items that you need for these activities.

_d_ **1.** do your hair   ___ **5.** shave

___ **2.** take a shower   ___ **6.** wash your hair

___ **3.** put on makeup   ___ **7.** brush your teeth

___ **4.** do your nails

3. Look at the checklist. Check (✓) the items that Teresa packed.

Travel Packing List

☑ blow dryer	☐ mascara
☐ bobby pins	☐ mouthwash
☐ brush	☐ nail clipper
☐ cologne/perfume	☐ nail polish
☐ comb	☐ shampoo
☐ conditioner	☐ shaving cream
☐ curling iron	☐ shower cap
☐ dental floss	☐ soap
☐ deodorant	☐ sunscreen
☐ electric shaver/razor	☐ talcum powder
☐ emery board	☐ toothbrush
☐ lipstick	☐ toothpaste

4. Teresa is at a hotel. Look at the items the hotel gives guests. Go back to the checklist in Exercise 3. Check (✓) the additional items that Teresa now has.

5. What does Teresa still need? Complete her shopping list.

HOTEL KENT

To Buy

bobby pins

6. What about you? Which items do you use? Check (✓) the correct column.

	EVERY DAY	SOMETIMES	NEVER
sunscreen			
cologne			
conditioner			
hair spray			
dental floss			
body lotion			
moisturizer			
Other: _____			

Challenge List the personal hygiene items you take with you when you travel.

Symptoms and Injuries

1. Look in your dictionary. **True** or **False**?

   a. The woman in bed has chills. _____True_____

   b. The man in 11 has an insect bite on his right arm. _____

   c. The man in 13 has a cut on his thumb. _____

   d. The man in 14 didn't use enough sunscreen. _____

   e. The man in 15 has a blister on his left hand. _____

   f. The young man with a handkerchief has a bloody nose. _____

   g. The woman in 18 sprained her right ankle. _____

2. Look at Tania's medicine. Complete the form. (You can look at **page 81** in your dictionary for help.)

   COUGHEX · FOR DENTAL PAIN · Antacid · LOZENGES · CLEAR NOSE · Pharmacy Dr williams RX#669016 Tania Zobor APPLY TO SKIN

Patient's name:	_____Tania Zobor_____

   Please check (✓) all the symptoms you have.

   I often get...
   ☐ headaches   ☐ earaches   ☑ toothaches   ☐ stomachaches   ☐ backaches
   ☐ sore throats   ☐ nasal congestion   ☐ fevers   ☐ bruises   ☐ rashes

   I often...
   ☐ cough   ☐ sneeze   ☐ feel naseous   ☐ feel dizzy   ☐ vomit

3. What about you? Complete the form for yourself or someone you know.

   Patient's name: _____

   Please check (✓) all the symptoms you have.

   I often get...
   ☐ headaches   ☐ earaches   ☐ toothaches   ☐ stomachaches   ☐ backaches
   ☐ sore throats   ☐ nasal congestion   ☐ fevers   ☐ bruises   ☐ rashes

   I often...
   ☐ cough   ☐ sneeze   ☐ feel naseous   ☐ feel dizzy   ☐ vomit

   Challenge What can you do for the health problems in Exercise 3? **Example:** *headaches—take pain reliever*

1. Look at the bottom picture in your dictionary. Write the name of the part of the body.

    a. asthma   <u>lungs</u>   **d.** TB   _____

    b. high blood pressure _____   **e.** intestinal parasites _____

    c. diabetes   _____   **f.** HIV   _____

2. Look at the photos of Mehmet when he was a child. Complete the form.

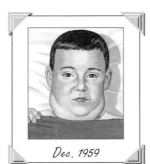

Nov. 1951   *Jan. 1953*   *Dec. 1959*   *May 1964*

Name <u>Mehmet Caner</u>   Date of birth <u>April 18, 1949</u>

Check (✓) the illnesses or conditions you had as a child.

    ☐ measles   ☐ chicken pox   ☐ mumps

    ☐ asthma   ☐ allergies   ☑ ear infections

3. What about you? Complete the form for yourself or someone you know.

Name _____   Date of birth _____

Check (✓) the illnesses or conditions you had as a child.

    ☐ measles   ☐ chicken pox   ☐ mumps

    ☐ asthma   ☐ allergies   ☐ ear infections

Challenge List the things you do when you have a cold or the flu. **Example:** *drink hot water with lemon*

Health Care

1. Look in your dictionary. Who said…?

a. **Your prescription is ready.** _pharmacist_

b. **The brace is helping you walk better.** _____

c. **These glasses will look nice on you.** _____

d. **This hearing aid will help.** _____

e. **This cast stays on for six weeks.** _____

2. Look at Dr. Burns's notes for Brian, a patient injured in an accident. **True** or **False**?

From the desk of
Dr. Mary Burns

1. Use heating pad on arm.
2. Take over-the-counter pain reliever when needed.
3. Exercise every day.
4. Fill prescription for tetracycline.
5. Use cane for 4 weeks.
6. Call for appointment in 2 weeks.

a. This is a prescription. _False_

b. Brian must get bed rest. _____

c. He can't exercise. _____

d. He can use a heating pad. _____

e. He needs a humidifier. _____

f. He must take medicine. _____

g. He needs crutches. _____

3. Look at the bar graph. Complete the sentences.

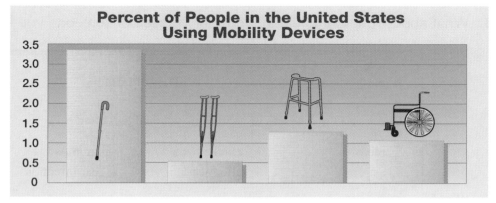

Based on information from the U.S. National Center for Health Statistics, 1992.

a. 0.51% of people in the U.S. use _crutches_ .

b. 1.29% use a _____ .

c. 1.08% use a _____ .

d. 3.35% use a _____ .

4. Look at the picture. Circle the words to complete the statements.

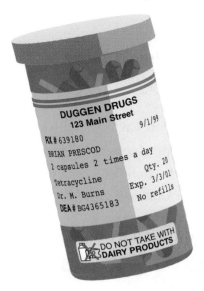

a. Brian went to the <u>chiropractor</u> /(<u>pharmacy</u>.)

b. He got <u>over-the-counter medication</u> / <u>prescription medication</u>.

c. The bottle contains <u>capsules</u> / <u>tablets</u>.

d. The <u>prescription label</u> / <u>warning label</u> reads "Do not take with dairy products."

e. Brian can't <u>drink fluids</u> / <u>eat cheese</u> with this medicine.

f. The <u>dosage</u> / <u>expiration date</u> is two pills twice a day.

g. The medicine isn't good after <u>September 1999</u> / <u>March 2001</u>.

5. What about you? Check (✓) the items you <u>think</u> are in your medicine cabinet. Then check your answers at home.

☐ pain reliever

☐ cold tablets

☐ antacid

☐ vitamins

☐ cough syrup

☐ throat lozenges

☐ nasal spray

☐ ointment

☐ eyedrops

☐ Other: _____

Challenge Look at some prescription or over-the-counter medication in your medicine cabinet. What's the dosage? The expiration date? Is there a warning label? Make a list.

Medical Emergencies

1. Look in your dictionary. **True** or **False**?

   a. The girl under the blue blanket is injured.   _____True_____

   b. The man in the yellow shirt is hurt, too.   _____

   c. The man in the red shirt is having an allergic reaction.   _____

   d. The child in the swimming pool is unconscious.   _____

   e. The woman at the table is choking on a fish bone.   _____

   f. The boy in the doctor's office broke a leg.   _____

2. Look at the chart. How did the people injure themselves? Circle the correct words.

NUMBER OF INJURIES IN THE UNITED STATES IN A YEAR	
PRODUCT	**ESTIMATED INJURIES**
stairs, steps	1,055,355
knives	460,625
bathtubs, showers	151,852
drugs, medications	115,814
hot water	43,457
TVs	36,457
pesticides	16,281

Based on information from the Consumer Product Safety Commission, 1994.

Maybe people....

   drowned /(fell)
   a.

   bled / couldn't breathe
   b.

   broke bones / had heart attacks
   c.

   got frostbite / overdosed
   d.

   burned themselves / choked
   e.

   were in shock / got an electric shock
   f.

   swallowed poison / overdosed
   g.

3. What about you? Check (✓) the emergencies that have happened to you. When or where did they happen?

EMERGENCY	WHEN?/WHERE?
☐ I had an allergic reaction to _____.	_____
☐ I got frostbite.	_____
☐ I fell.	_____
☐ I broke my _____.	_____
☐ Other: _____.	_____

Challenge Write a paragraph about an emergency in Exercise 3. What treatment did you get? Look at **page 83** in your dictionary for help.

1. Look in your dictionary. Write the first aid item for these conditions.

    a. broken finger   _splint_

    b. rash on hand

    c. swollen foot   or

    d. infected cut   or

2. Look at the items from Chen's first aid kit. Check (✓) the items he has.

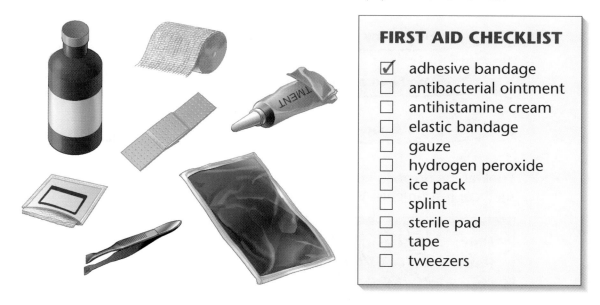

FIRST AID CHECKLIST

- ☑ adhesive bandage
- ☐ antibacterial ointment
- ☐ antihistamine cream
- ☐ elastic bandage
- ☐ gauze
- ☐ hydrogen peroxide
- ☐ ice pack
- ☐ splint
- ☐ sterile pad
- ☐ tape
- ☐ tweezers

3. What about you? Check (✓) the first aid items you <u>think</u> you have at home. Then check your answers at home.

FIRST AID CHECKLIST

- ☐ adhesive bandage
- ☐ antibacterial ointment
- ☐ antihistamine cream
- ☐ elastic bandage
- ☐ gauze
- ☐ hydrogen peroxide
- ☐ ice pack
- ☐ splint
- ☐ sterile pad
- ☐ tape
- ☐ tweezers

DO YOU KNOW HOW TO DO...?	YES	NO
the Heimlich maneuver		
CPR		
rescue breathing		

Challenge   Look at the items in Exercise 3. What can you use them for? **Example:**
adhesive bandages—cuts

Clinics

1. Look in your dictionary. Who said…?

   a. **Your pressure is very good.** _____nurse_____

   b. **I'll give you an insurance form, Mr. Sun.** _____

   c. **In a month, no more braces, Ryan!** _____

   d. **Here's my insurance card.** _____

   e. **You have one more cavity.** _____

   f. **Good-bye tartar!** _____

2. Look at the doctor's notes. What did the doctor use? Match the notes with the medical instruments. Write the number.

   Date: 3/5/02
   Patient: Carla Vega
   1. weight—135 lbs.
   2. B.P. — 120/80
   3. temp.— 98.6°
   4. lungs—clear
   5. vision—20/20
      (doesn't need glasses)
   6. gave flu vaccination

   ____ a. syringe
   ____ b. eye chart
   _1_ c. scale
   ____ d. thermometer
   ____ e. blood pressure gauge
   ____ f. stethoscope

3. What about you? Think of the last time you saw the doctor. How long were you…?

   in the waiting room   _____

   in the examining room   _____

   on the examination table   _____

Challenge Find out about health insurance in other countries. Which countries have national health insurance? Who can get it?

1. Look in your dictionary. **True** or **False**?

   a. Picture A: The man is making an appointment to see the doctor.   _True_

   b. Picture B: The nurse is checking the patient's blood pressure.   _____

   c. Picture C: The doctor is examining the patient's mouth.   _____

   d. Picture F: The doctor is looking in the patient's ears.   _____

   e. Picture K: The dentist is drilling a tooth.   _____

2. Write the words under the correct pictures.

clean teeth	draw blood	examine eyes	fill a cavity
give a shot	pull a tooth	take an X ray	~~take temperature~~

a. _take temperature_

b. _____

c. _____

d. _____

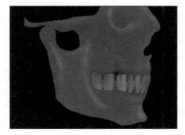

e. _____

f. _____

g. _____

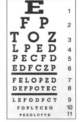

h. _____

Challenge Look at **page 184** in this book. Complete the diagram.

A Hospital

1. Look at the patient's room in your dictionary. What should a patient use who...?

   a. wants to eat breakfast   _bed table_

   b. wants to sit up in the hospital bed   _____

   c. doesn't have pajamas   _____

   d. can't walk to the bathroom   _____

   e. wants a nurse   _____

2. Look at the two lists. Match the patients with the hospital staff. Write the number.

	PATIENTS			4/7/01
	Name	**Age**	**Room**	**Condition**
_2_	**a.** Ellen Lee	25	243	pregnant
____	**b.** Tom Lyons	17	265	nervous, confused
____	**c.** Chris Baker	6	284	chicken pox
____	**d.** Allen Rogers	80	364	eye pain
____	**e.** Marta Varga	53	398	diabetes *requested clean sheets*
____	**f.** Tony Petchak	49	298	HIV *blood test scheduled*
____	**g.** Arthur Lewin	75	376	heart attack
____	**h.** Ilsa Grueber	63	378	intestinal parasites
____	**i.** Annie Minkoff	78	249	broken hip *X rays scheduled*

HOSPITAL STAFF		4/7/01
1.	Dr. James Cranston	internist
2.	Dr. Mary Ferguson	obstetrician
3.	Dr. Robert Hecht	ophthalmologist
4.	Dr. Carmen Rivera	pediatrician
5.	Dr. Doug London	psychiatrist
6.	Dr. Mei-hua Chang	cardiologist
7.	Charlie Olsen	X-ray technician
8.	Joan Osborne	lab technician
9.	Billy Parker	orderly

3. Look in your dictionary. Who's…?

    a. standing near the vital signs monitor   *nurse*

    b. taking flowers to a patient   _____

    c. carrying a medication tray   _____

    d. talking to the dietician   _____

    e. pushing a gurney   _____

    f. lying on the operating table   _____

    g. wearing glasses   _____

    h. helping the surgeon   _____

    i. in the operating room with the surgeon and the nurse   _____

4. Match the objects in the supply room with the items on the supplies list. Write the number.

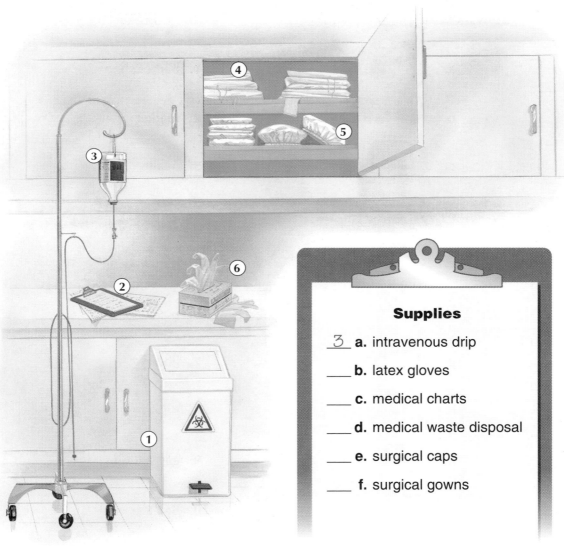

Supplies

   3 **a.** intravenous drip

   ___ **b.** latex gloves

   ___ **c.** medical charts

   ___ **d.** medical waste disposal

   ___ **e.** surgical caps

   ___ **f.** surgical gowns

Challenge Find out the names of an internist, an ophthalmologist, and a pediatrician in your community. Make a list.

▶ **Go to page 175 for Another Look (Unit 6).**

City Streets

1. Look in your dictionary. Circle the correct words to complete the sentences.
   a. There's a (furniture store)/ hardware store on Main and Elm.
   b. There's a movie theater / an office building on First and Elm.
   c. The mosque / synagogue is on Second and Oak.
   d. The car dealership / parking garage is next to the high-rise building.
   e. The fire station / police station is on Main and Oak.
   f. There's a hotel / motel on Pine and Second.
   g. The city hall / courthouse is on Main and Pine.
   h. There's a woman in front of the bakery / bank.

2. Match the pictures with the places. Write the number.

   _2_ **a.**   **1.** barber shop

   ___ **b.**   **2.** market

   ___ **c.**   **3.** health club

   ___ **d.**   **4.** bank

   ___ **e.**   **5.** hardware store

   ___ **f.**   **6.** post office

   ___ **g.**   **7.** library

   ___ **h.**   **8.** park

   ___ **i.**   **9.** gas station

   ___ **j.**   **10.** theater

   ___ **k.**   **11.** coffee shop

   ___ **l.**   **12.** fire station

3. Look at the map. Complete the notes.

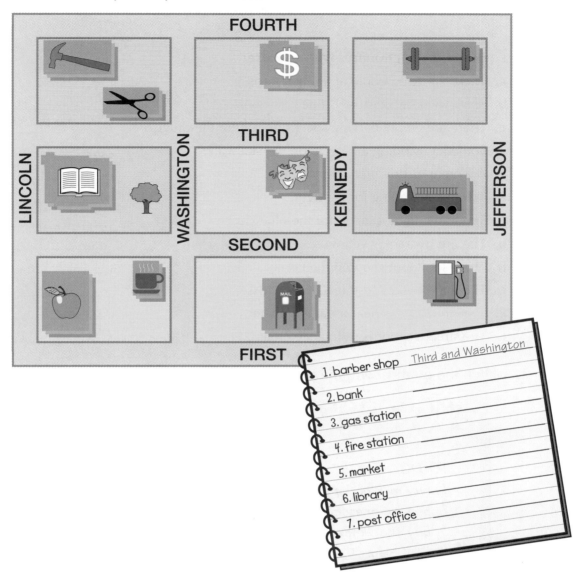

1. barber shop _Third and Washington_
2. bank _____
3. gas station _____
4. fire station _____
5. market _____
6. library _____
7. post office _____

4. What about you? Write the street locations for these places in your community.

school   _____

library   _____

post office   _____

hospital   _____

fire station   _____

police station   _____

Other: _____

Challenge   Draw a street map of an area you know. Include the location of some places from Exercise 2.

An Intersection

1. Look in your dictionary. **True** or **False**?

   a. There are two people at the bus stop. _____True_____

   b. The convenience store is open 24 hours. _____

   c. There are empty parking spaces in front of the drugstore. _____

   d. Someone is riding a bicycle on the sidewalk. _____

   e. A woman is driving a gray car. _____

   f. The bus is waiting for the light. _____

   g. The traffic light is green for the blue car. _____

   h. The fire hydrant is yellow. _____

   i. There's a donut shop on the corner. _____

   j. There are two pedestrians in the crosswalk. _____

   k. The streetlight is near a parking meter. _____

   l. The street vendor is selling ice cream. _____

2. Match the errands with the places. Write the number.

   TO DO:
   1. buy milk and eggs
   2. pick up prescription
   3. buy the Times
   4. mail rent
   5. meet Meng for lunch
   6. pick up raincoat
   7. drop off roll of film
   8. copy English paper
   9. wash sheets and towels
   10. call Olga at 5:30

   ____ **a.** photo shop

   ____ **b.** public telephone

   ____ **c.** dry cleaners

   ____ **d.** copy center

   ____ **e.** drugstore

   ____ **f.** Laundromat

   _1_ **g.** convenience store

   ____ **h.** fast food restaurant

   ____ **i.** newsstand

   ____ **j.** mailbox

3. Cross out the word that doesn't belong.

a. **People**	pedestrian	street vendor	~~corner~~
b. **Stores**	donut shop	mailbox	pharmacy
c. **Services**	bicycle	Laundromat	nail salon
d. **Transportation**	parking space	bus	motorcycle
e. **Parts of the street**	curb	crosswalk	drive-thru window
f. **Things you put coins in**	public telephone	parking meter	fire hydrant
g. **Things that move**	sign	cart	garbage truck

4. Write the location of these signs. Use words from Exercise 3.

a. _____Laundromat_____

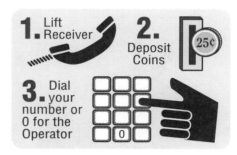

b. _____

c. _____

d. _____

French Fries.....................$1.00
   with cheese....................$1.50
Hamburger.......................$3.00
Cheeseburger....................$3.50
   Lettuce & Tomato.............50¢
Popcorn...........................$1.35
Gum................................65¢

e. _____

First Mail pick-up	8:30 AM
Next pick-up	10:30 AM
Next pick-up	1:30 PM
Next pick-up	4:30 PM
Final Mail pick-up	7:30 PM

f. _____

5. What about you? Make a list of neighborhood errands and locations. Use your own paper.

Example: *pick up prescription—drugstore*

Challenge   Look in your dictionary. Write the locations of five stores. **Example:** *The donut shop is on the corner.*

91

A Mall

1. Look in your dictionary. Where can you buy these items? Do not use *department store*.

a. ___card store___   b. _____   c. _____

d. _____   e. _____   f. _____

g. _____   h. _____   i. _____

2. Look in your dictionary. Complete the mall directory.

MALL DIRECTORY

Cards/Books	Floor	Services	Floor
card store	1	optician	
Department Store	1, 2		
Entertainment/Music		**Shoes/Accessories**	
Food		**Specialty Stores**	
		pet store	

3. Look at this mall directory and map. Circle the words to complete the conversations.

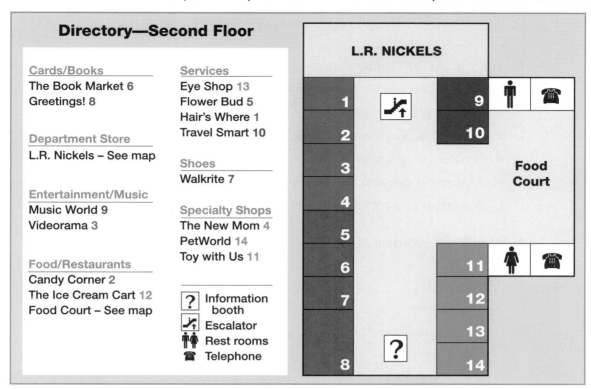

Customer 1: Excuse me. Where's the bookstore?

Information: It's next to the <u>pet store</u> (shoe store.)
                                    a.

Customer 2: Can you tell me where the hair salon is?

Information: Sure. It's next to the <u>department store / information booth</u>.
                                                          b.

Customer 3: I'm looking for the <u>escalator / women's rest room</u>.
                                          c.

Information: It's in front of Nickel's.

Customer 4: Hi. Where's the travel agency, please?

Information: It's right over there. Next to the <u>toy store / music store</u>.
                                                            d.

Customer 5: Excuse me. I'm looking for the candy store.

Information: It's between the <u>music store / video store</u> and the <u>hair salon / maternity shop</u>.
                                               e.   **f.**

Customer 6: Excuse me. Is there an optician in this mall?

Information: Yes. There's one across from the <u>card store / candy store</u>.
                                                          g.

Challenge   Look at the map in Exercise 3. Write the locations of Videorama, the men's rest room, Flower Bud, and PetWorld.

1. Look at the top picture in your dictionary. **True** or **False**?

   a. A childcare worker is dropping off a little girl.   <u>False</u>

   b. A girl is playing with toys.   <u>   </u>

   c. The girl in blue jeans is taking a nap.   <u>   </u>

   d. A parent is changing diapers.   <u>   </u>

   e. A parent is dressing his son.   <u>   </u>

   f. A woman in a rocking chair is reading a story.   <u>   </u>

2. Match the words that go together. Write the number.

   <u>4</u> **a.** high   **1.** ring

   ___ **b.** diaper   **2.** table

   ___ **c.** teething   **3.** pin

   ___ **d.** cloth   **4.** chair

   ___ **e.** changing   **5.** diaper

3. What is it? Complete the sentences. Use the words from Exercise 2.

   a. A baby sits in it.   <u>a high chair</u>

   b. A baby puts it in its mouth.   <u>   </u>

   c. A disposable diaper doesn't need it.   <u>   </u>

   d. A baby lies on it.   <u>   </u>

   e. A baby wears it.   <u>   </u>

4. What about you? Have you ever…? Check (✓) the correct column.

	YES	NO
held a baby		
read a story to a child		
fed a child		
dressed a child		
changed a diaper		
rocked a baby to sleep		

5. Cross out the word that doesn't belong. You can use your dictionary for help.

a.	**People**	parent	childcare worker	~~pacifier~~
b.	**Places to sit**	high chair	diaper pail	potty seat
c.	**Things a baby wears**	walker	bib	diaper
d.	**Things to feed a baby**	formula	baby food	disinfectant
e.	**Things that have wheels**	rocking chair	carriage	stroller
f.	**Things to put in a baby's mouth**	teething ring	cubby	nipple
g.	**Things for changing diapers**	baby powder	playpen	wipes
h.	**Things a baby plays with**	baby backpack	rattles	toys
i.	**Things that hold a baby**	diaper pins	baby carrier	car safety seat

6. There are 12 childcare words. They go → and ↓. Find and circle them.

C	A	R	R	I	A	G	E	H
U	N	A	I	W	I	P	E	S
B	T	T	F	A	O	A	O	T
B	O	T	T	L	E	C	N	R
Y	Y	L	R	K	P	I	I	O
R	P	L	M	E	L	F	P	L
Y	B	E	U	R	E	I	P	L
D	I	A	P	E	R	E	L	E
I	B	I	A	C	I	R	E	R

Challenge Rewrite the false sentences in Exercise 1. Make them true.

95

U.S. Mail

1. Look in your dictionary. **True** or **False**?

   a. The letter carrier delivers mail.   True

   b. The postcard has a return address.   _____

   c. You can send a package by parcel post.   _____

   d. The air letter is white.   _____

   e. You can receive Express Mail the next day. _____

2. Circle the correct words to complete the sentences.

   a. The envelope is <u>blue</u> /(<u>white</u>.)

   b. This is a <u>greeting card</u> / <u>letter</u>.

   c. The <u>mailing address</u> / <u>return address</u> is 65 River Dr., Cleveland, OH 44103.

   d. The <u>postage</u> / <u>postmark</u> says December 15.

   e. Alicia sent this <u>priority mail</u> / <u>certified mail</u>.

3. What about you? Address this envelope to your teacher. Use your school's address. Don't forget your return address.

Challenge Find out how much it costs to send a letter, a postcard, and an aerogramme.

1. Look in your dictionary. Circle the words to complete the sentences.

  a. The security guard / (teller) is speaking to a man.

  b. The man has cash / a passbook in his hand.

  c. The ATM / vault is behind the teller.

  d. The checkbook / safe-deposit box is light green.

  e. The deposit slip is about the same size as the ATM card / checkbook.

2. Look at the bank receipt. **True** or **False**?

  a. This is a monthly statement. _____False_____

  b. The customer used an ATM. _____

  c. She made a deposit. _____

  d. She withdrew $100 from her checking account. _____

  e. Her savings account number is 056588734. _____

  f. Her balance is $623.40. _____

FIRST BANK

54 CHURCH STREET
LIBERTYVILLE, IL

DATE: 05/06/99   TIME: 11:51
ATM : 045-3
CARD NUMBER: **************6434

TRANSACTION: WITHDRAWAL
SERIAL NUM.:   345
AMOUNT: $100.00
FROM SAVINGS: 056588734
BALANCE: $6,234

3. Imagine you want to transfer forty dollars from your savings account to your checking account. Look at the ATM screens. Circle the correct transaction for each screen.

a.

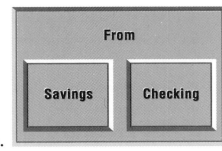

b.

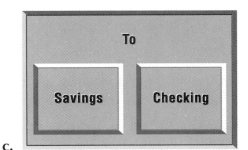

c.

d.

Challenge Rewrite the false sentences in Exercise 2. Make them true.

A Library

1. Look in your dictionary. Where can you find...?

   a. titles and locations of library books   in the   <u>online catalog</u>

                                                               or   _____

   b. magazines and newspapers   in the   _____

   c. maps   in an   _____

   d. records and CDs   in the   _____

   e. the library clerk   at the   _____

   f. the reference librarian   at the   _____

2. Look at the chart. Complete the sentences.

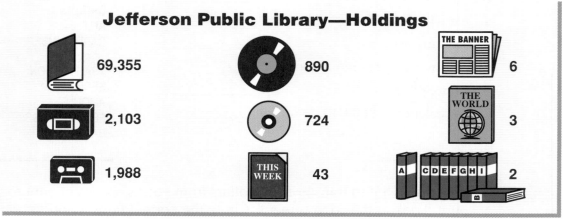

   a. There are 724 <u>compact discs</u> in the library.

   b. The library has 43 different kinds of _____ and 6 different kinds of

       _____ .

   c. There are 3 _____ .

   d. The library has almost 70,000 _____ .

   e. There are 2 sets of _____ .

   f. The library has almost 2,000_____ and a little more than 2,000

       _____ .

   g. There are almost 900 _____ .

3. What about you? Check (✓) the items you would like to borrow from a library.

   ☐ books   ☐ records   ☐ CDs

   ☐ audiocassettes   ☐ videocassettes   ☐ Other: _____

Challenge Go to your school library or a local library. Where are the items you checked in Exercise 3? For how long can you borrow them?

1. Look in your dictionary. Circle the words to complete the sentences.

   a. The guard / (police officer) arrested the suspect.

   b. The suspect / witness wears handcuffs.

   c. The defense attorney / prosecuting attorney is a man.

   d. The court reporter / judge says "guilty."

   e. There are ten / twelve people on the jury.

   f. The convict / bailiff is in prison.

2. Complete the sentences with the words in the box. Then number the events in order.

court	defendant	~~jail~~	lawyer	released
	suspect	trial	verdict	

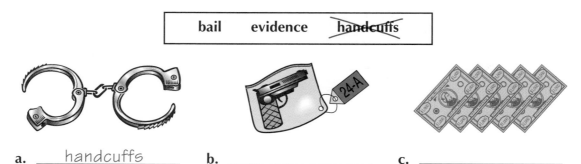

_____ **a.** The defendant goes to _____jail_____.

_____ **b.** The defendant stands _____.

_____ **c.** The judge sentences the _____.

_____ **d.** The defendant appears in _____.

_____ **e.** The convict is _____.

_____ **f.** The judge gives the _____.

_1_ **g.** The police officer arrests a _____.

_____ **h.** The suspect hires a _____.

3. Label the items. Use the words in the box.

bail	evidence	~~handcuffs~~

a. ____handcuffs____   **b.** _____   **c.** _____

_____ **Challenge** Look in your dictionary. Tell the story. **Begin:** *The police officer arrested the suspect…*

Crime

1. Look in your dictionary. Read the TV movie descriptions. Circle all the crime words.

> ❷ **Under the Influence ('89)** Forrest March, Jill Gilmore. (Drunk driving) destroys two families.
>
> ❹ **The Necklace ('95)** Rob Philip, Seth Jackson. A burglary changes life in a small, quiet town.
>
> ❺ **Crimes Against Property ('99)** Anna Lauck, Sam Hull, Evan Scott. A family is shocked when their teenage son is arrested for vandalism.
>
> ❼ **The Victim ('88)** Elisa Rivera, Bill Delany. Woman fights back during a mugging.
>
> ❾ **The Candy Shop ('93)** Tom Ryder, Amara Dee. Police find teenagers selling illegal drugs.
>
> ⓭ **Keep the Change ('97)** Liza Moore, Dean Adams. A brutal assault changes a man's life.
>
> ㉘ **East Side Saga ('93)** Brian Terry, Johnny Ray Lone. A story of gang violence.
>
> ㊶ **The Last Breakfast ('90)** Lon Matheson, Verna Tiler. A doctor is arrested for her husband's murder.

2. Match the TV movies with the descriptions in Exercise 1. Write the channel number.

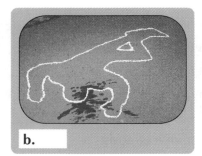

a. 28

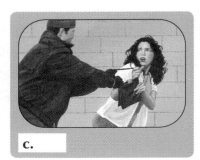

b.

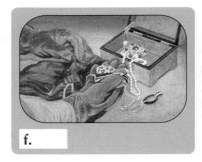

c.

d.

e.

f.

g.

h.

Challenge Look at the TV listings in a newspaper or TV program guide. Which programs are about crimes? Which types of crimes?

1. Look in your dictionary. **True** or **False**?

   a. The girls on the street are friends.   _True_

   b. The women on the subway are holding their purses close to their bodies. _____

   c. The elderly woman is opening the door to a stranger. _____

   d. The taxi driver is drinking and driving. _____

   e. The elderly man is reporting a crime. _____

2. Match the problems with the advice. Write the number.

_5_ **a.**

1.   Hold your purse close to your body!

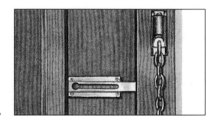

___ **b.**

2.   Walk with a friend!

___ **c.**

3.   Protect your wallet!

___ **d.**

4.   Lock your door!

___ **e.**

5.   Stay on well-lit streets!

Challenge   Make a list of steps you take to be safe in public.

1. Look in your dictionary. Write the disaster or emergency.

a. (It's covering the house!)　　　　_mudslide_

b. (It's going to hit the farm!)　　　　_____

c. (We need rain.)　　　　_____

d. (Don't move. We're coming to get you!)　　　　_____

e. (The light was red! You didn't stop!)　　　　_____

f. (Mindy! Mindy! Where are you, Mindy?)　　　　_____

g. (There's almost a foot of snow!)　　　　_____

2. Look at the chart.

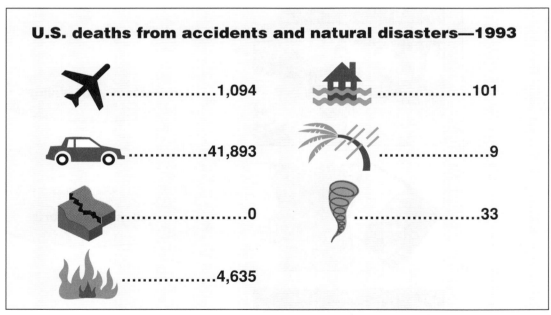

U.S. deaths from accidents and natural disasters—1993

✈ 1,094	🏠〰 101
🚗 41,893	🌴 9
▨ 0	🌀 33
🔥 4,635	

Based on information from: *Statistical Abstracts of the United States, 1996–1997.* (U.S. Census Bureau)

Number the disasters in order of how many people died. (Number 1 = the most deaths)

___ fire　　　　___ airplane crash　　　　___ tornado　　　　___ flood

___ earthquake　　　　___ hurricane　　　　_1_ car accident

3. Match the photos with the newspaper headlines. Write the number.

 3 **a.**

___ **b.**

___ **c.**

___ **d.**

___ **e.**

1. Explosion Rocks City Center

2. Search and Rescue Team Does the Job

3. Tidal Wave Hits Japan

4. Fire Fighters Fight Flames

5. Volcanic Eruption At Mt. St. Helens

4. What about you? Which natural disasters have you experienced? Complete the chart.

	WHERE?	WHEN?
earthquake		
blizzard		
hurricane		
tornado		
flood		
Other: _____		

Challenge Find information about a natural disaster. Look in an almanac, an encyclopedia, or a newspaper. What kind of disaster was it? Where and when did it happen?

▶ **Go to page 176 for Another Look (Unit 7).**

1. Look in your dictionary. How many ... can you see?

    a. people at the bus stop   _2_   **c.** taxis at the taxi stand   _____

    b. passengers on the bus   _____   **d.** buses on the ferry   _____

2. Cross out the word that doesn't belong.

a. Types of transportation	bus	ferry	subway	~~ticket~~
b. People	bus driver	passenger	transfer	conductor
c. Forms of payment	fare	track	token	fare card
d. Places to wait	passenger	platform	bus stop	train station
e. Things to read	schedule	train	route	meter

3. Look at the bar graph.

Average One-Way Trip from Home to Work

Based on information from the U.S. Department of Energy and Transportation, 1991.

Match the transportation with the average distance.

  _3_ **a.** walk   **1.** about 7 miles

  ___ **b.** bus   **2.** about 25 miles

  ___ **c.** train   **3.** less than 1 mile

  ___ **d.** subway   **4.** about 3 miles

  ___ **e.** taxi   **5.** about 9 miles

4. What about you? What form of transportation do you take to go to...?

    a. school   _____   **c.** the market   _____

    b. work   _____   **d.** Other: _____

Challenge Look at **page 184** in this book. Follow the instructions.

1. Look in your dictionary. **True** or **False**?

    a. The ferry is going under the bridge.   _False_

    b. A woman is getting into the taxi.   _____

    c. A man is getting out of the front of the taxi.   _____

    d. A red car is getting onto the highway.   _____

    e. A green car is getting off the highway.   _____

    f. There are two people going down the stairs.   _____

    g. A taxi is going through the tunnel.   _____

2. Look at the map. Circle the correct words to complete the directions.

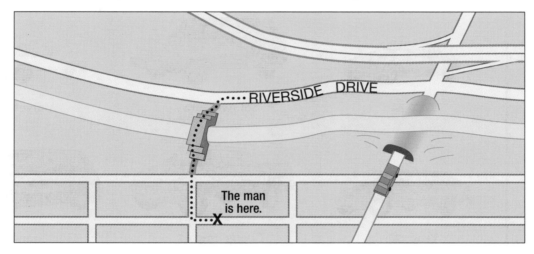

The man is here.

Man: Excuse me. How do I get to Riverside Drive?

Woman: Riverside Drive? Go around the (corner) / tunnel. Then go down / up the
                                                   a.   **b.**

        stairs and over / under the bridge / highway. Go down / up the stairs and you'll
                          c.   **d.**   **e.**

        be right on Riverside Drive.

Man: Oh, so I have to go across / around the bridge?
                                        f.

Woman: That's right.

3. Read the conversation in Exercise 2 again. Circle the correct answer.

    The man is in a taxi / on a bus / walking.

_____ **Challenge** Write directions to get from your home to school.

Cars and Trucks

1. Look in your dictionary. Circle the correct words to complete the sentences.

    a. The compact / ~~subcompact~~ is red.

    b. The camper / station wagon is beige.

    c. The dump truck / tow truck has a red stripe.

    d. The moving van / tractor trailer has an orange cab.

2. Look at the chart. Match the car models with the kinds of cars. Write the number.

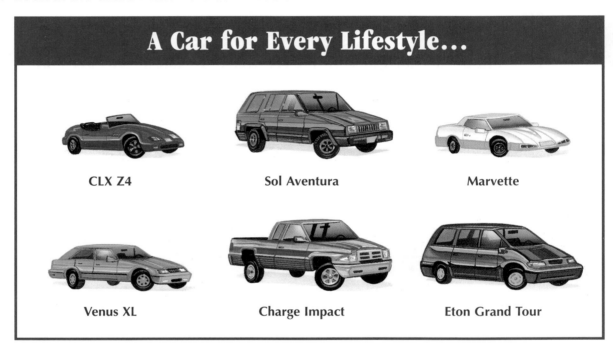

A Car for Every Lifestyle...

CLX Z4   Sol Aventura   Marvette

Venus XL   Charge Impact   Eton Grand Tour

<table>
<tr><td>_5_</td><td>**a.** Venus XL</td><td>**1.** minivan</td></tr>
<tr><td>___</td><td>**b.** Marvette</td><td>**2.** SUV</td></tr>
<tr><td>___</td><td>**c.** Charge Impact</td><td>**3.** pickup truck</td></tr>
<tr><td>___</td><td>**d.** Eton Grand Tour</td><td>**4.** sports car</td></tr>
<tr><td>___</td><td>**e.** Sol Aventura</td><td>**5.** midsize car</td></tr>
<tr><td>___</td><td>**f.** CLX Z4</td><td>**6.** convertible</td></tr>
</table>

3. What about you? Which car do you like? Choose one from Exercise 2.

    Color: _____   Model: _____

Challenge Explain your choice in Exercise 3. **Example:** *I like the Eton Grand Tour minivan because I have a big family.*

1. Look at the intersection on **pages 90 and 91** in your dictionary. **True** or **False**? (*Note:* The Burger Queen is on the southwest corner.)

a. Mel's Donuts is on the northeast corner. _____True_____

b. The convertible is going west. _____

c. The bicycle is going east. _____

d. The bus is going north. _____

e. The dry cleaners and the nail salon are on the same block. _____

f. There's a stop sign at the intersection. _____

g. There's a "no parking" sign near the park. _____

h. There's a pedestrian crossing sign at the northwest corner. _____

i. The motorcycle is on a one-way street. _____

j. There's handicapped parking in front of the dry cleaners. _____

k. There aren't any speed limit signs. _____

2. Look at the map. Use your pen or pencil to follow the directions to a shoe store. Put an X on the shoe store.

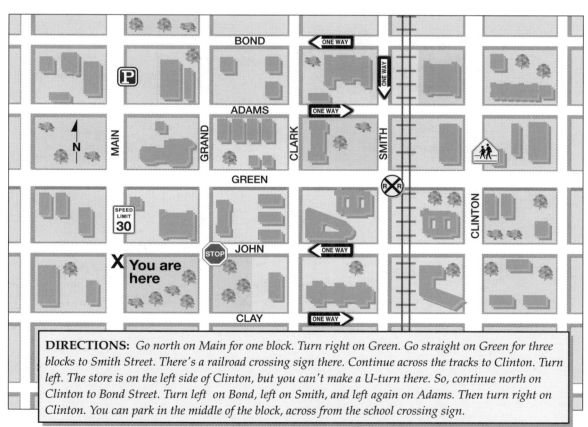

DIRECTIONS: *Go north on Main for one block. Turn right on Green. Go straight on Green for three blocks to Smith Street. There's a railroad crossing sign there. Continue across the tracks to Clinton. Turn left. The store is on the left side of Clinton, but you can't make a U-turn there. So, continue north on Clinton to Bond Street. Turn left on Bond, left on Smith, and left again on Adams. Then turn right on Clinton. You can park in the middle of the block, across from the school crossing sign.*

Challenge Give directions to a place near your school. Draw a map.

Parts of a Car and Car Maintenance

1. Look in your dictionary. What does the person need to use or check?

    a. Turn left!   _turn signal_

    b. It's raining.   _____

    c. It's hot in here.   _____

    d. The battery needs recharging.   _____

    e. Do we need gas?   _____

    f. That car doesn't see us!   _____

    g. You're going too slow.   _____

    h. Stop at the next traffic light.   _____

    i. It's cold in here.   _____

    j. How fast are you going?   _____

    k. What's the weather report for tomorrow? _____

    l. How many miles have we driven today? _____

2. Look at the diagram of a rental car. An X shows a problem. Look at the list and check (✓) all the car parts that have problems.

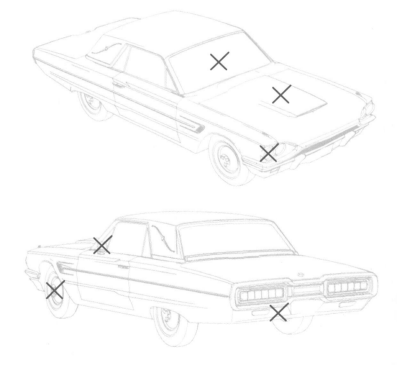

A&B Rental

- ☐ brake light
- ☑ bumper
- ☐ headlight
- ☐ hood
- ☐ hubcap
- ☐ license plate
- ☐ sideview mirror
- ☐ taillight
- ☐ tire
- ☐ trunk
- ☐ windshield

3. Label the car parts. Then match the parts with the problems. Write the number.

__2__ **a.** _____ tire _____

1. The car needs oil.

_____ **b.** _____

2. The tire needs air.

_____ **c.** _____

3. The battery needs recharging.

_____ **d.** _____

4. The car needs gas.

_____ **e.** _____

5. The radiator needs coolant.

4. What about you? Check (✓) the items you would like in a car.

☐ air bags ☐ child safety seat ☐ Other: _____

☐ air conditioning ☐ stick shift ☐ _____

☐ automatic transmission ☐ tape deck ☐ _____

Challenge Explain your choices in Exercise 4. Write sentences. **Example:** *I would like air conditioning because it's more comfortable.*

1. Look at the top picture in your dictionary. Answer the questions.

   a. How many passengers are in line at the check-in counter? _2_

   b. What's the gate number? _____

   c. What's the departure time? _____

   d. How many children are near the boarding area? _____

2. Circle the words to complete the sentences. Then write where the people are. Use the words in the box.

airline terminal	~~airplane~~	airplane
baggage claim area	cockpit	customs

   Passenger: Where's your luggage?

   Passenger: Up there. In the
   luggage carrier /(overhead compartment).   _airplane_
   a.

   Passenger: I feel nauseous.

   Flight attendant: Here's an <u>airsickness bag / oxygen mask</u>.   _____
   b.

   Passenger: I'm looking for the luggage from flight 371.

   Airline rep: It will be on that <u>carousel / helicopter</u>.   _____
   c.

   Passenger: Do you need help with that?

   Passenger: No, thanks. I have a
   <u>control tower / luggage carrier</u>.   _____
   d.

   Customs officer: Do you have anything to declare?

   Passenger: Yes. Here's my <u>declaration form / tray table</u>.   _____
   e.

   Pilot: This is your captain speaking. We will be at the
   <u>check-in counter / gate</u> in about seven minutes.   _____
   f.

Challenge Describe the airport in your dictionary. Write at least six sentences.

1. Look at page 111 in your dictionary. Complete the information for the passenger.

SKYAIR		
	Flight number:	508
	Destination:	
	Departure time:	
	Seat number:	

2. Look in your dictionary. What is the passenger doing? Use the *-ing* form of the verb.

a. Is this 14F? ___finding his seat___

b. Can I walk through now? _____

c. Here's $100. _____

d. There it is. Across the aisle. _____

e. This is making me feel sick. _____

f. Here it is! The large black one. _____

3. Look at the picture. Check (✓) the things the passenger did.

- ☑ got her boarding pass
- ☐ boarded the plane
- ☐ found her seat
- ☐ stowed her carry-on bag
- ☐ fastened her seat belt
- ☐ looked at the emergency card
- ☐ requested a pillow
- ☐ took off
- ☐ landed

Challenge List the things you can do to make a plane trip more comfortable. **Example:** *wear comfortable clothing*

▶ Go to page 177 for Another Look (Unit 8).

Types of Schools

1. Look in your dictionary. Where can you hear…?

a. It costs $10,000 a year.   _private school_

b. I love playing with blocks.   _____

c. How do you like UCLA?   _____

d. It looks like a church, Sister Mary.   _____

e. Our parents' taxes pay for it.   _____

f. That's the carburetor.   _____

2. Match the typical student age with the school. You can use your dictionary for help.

_2_ **a.** 20 years old   **1.** high school

___ **b.** 3 years old   **2.** college

___ **c.** 8 years old   **3.** preschool

___ **d.** 16 years old   **4.** middle school

___ **e.** 12 years old   **5.** elementary school

___ **f.** 30 years old   **6.** adult school

3. What about you? Complete the chart.

CHECK (✓) THE SCHOOLS YOU HAVE ATTENDED:	NAME	LOCATION	DATES
☐ elementary school			
☐ junior high school			
☐ high school			
☐ trade school			
☐ adult school			
☐ college/university			
☐ Other: _____			

Challenge Think of the different types of schools in another country. List in order the schools and the age of the typical student at each school.

1. Look in your dictionary. **True** or **False**?

    a. The writing assignment is due on October 3.   _____True_____

    b. The student is writing a first draft on his computer.   _____

    c. The student is editing his paper in red.   _____

    d. The student is getting feedback from another student.   _____

    e. The student is turning in his paper late.   _____

    f. The composition is about his job.   _____

    g. The final composition has more than one paragraph.   _____

2. Match the punctuation marks with the words. Write the number.

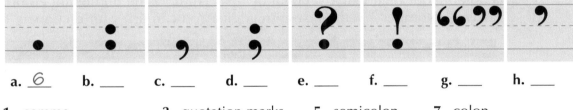

    a. _6_   **b.** ___   **c.** ___   **d.** ___   **e.** ___   **f.** ___   **g.** ___   **h.** ___

1. comma	**3.** quotation marks	**5.** semicolon	**7.** colon
2. exclamation mark	**4.** apostrophe	**6.** period	**8.** question mark

3. Look at the composition. Circle and correct four more punctuation mistakes.

> Name: Sonia Hernandez
>
> We're moving to San Diego(;) California next
> September. Im worried. Will I like it? Where
> will we live. My father says, "Don't worry.'
> He says that I'll make new friends. My mother
> says that soon San Diego will feel like home.
> "But I'm happy here?" I exclaim. I watch my
> father's face and listen to my mother's words.
> I feel better.

4. What about you? How did you and your family feel the last time you moved? Write five sentences. Underline all the adjectives.

    Example: *I felt <u>excited</u>.*

Challenge Write a paper about your life in this country. Edit your paper. Get feedback. Rewrite your paper and turn it in to your teacher.

1. Look in your dictionary. Circle the event that happened first.

   a. (Declaration of Independence)/ Civil War

   b. U.S. war with Mexico / Spanish American War

   c. first sound pictures / first air flight

   d. World War II / The Depression

   e. Bell invents the telephone / Edison invents the lightbulb

   f. King's assassination / Kennedy's assassination

   g. U.S. buys Louisiana / U.S. buys Alaska

   h. Cuban immigration to the U.S. / Hungarian immigration to the U.S.

2. Look in your dictionary. Who came first? Number the immigrant groups in order of arrival. (Number 1 = the first immigrants) You can use your dictionary for help.

IMMIGRATION TO THE UNITED STATES	
___ Chinese and Scandinavians	___ Middle Easterners and Central Americans
___ Cubans	_1_ English
___ Southeast Asians	___ Puerto Ricans
___ first group of Hungarians	___ Russians
___ Japanese	___ Armenians, Southern and Eastern Europeans
___ Filipinos	___ World War II refugees
___ second group of Irish	___ Koreans
___ Mexicans	___ Haitians
___ Spanish	___ Scots, Irish, Germans

3. Match the event with the category. Write the number.

   _2_ a. **WOMEN GET THE RIGHT TO VOTE**

   ___ b. **WASHINGTON** Becomes First President

   ___ c. *Cubans Come to the U.S.*

   ___ d. **ARMSTRONG LANDS ON THE MOON**

   ___ e. First Model A Ford Car

   1. invention

   2. movement

   3. election

   4. exploration

   5. immigration

4. Look in your dictionary. Label the events. Write the year in the box.

1776

a. <u>Declaration of Independence</u>

b. _____

c. _____

d. _____

e. _____

f. _____

5. What about you? Check (✔) the events you know about. Circle the events you want to learn more about.

☐ Cherokee Trail of Tears   ☐ war in Vietnam   ☐ abolition of slavery

☐ first air flight   ☐ Bill of Rights   ☐ civil rights movement

☐ Other: _____

_____ **Challenge** Choose an event from Exercise 5. Look in an encyclopedia or history book. Write a paragraph about the event. Try to answer these questions: Who was there? When did it happen? Where did it happen? Why did it happen?

U.S. Government and Citizenship

1. Look at the top of the page in your dictionary. Complete the diagram.

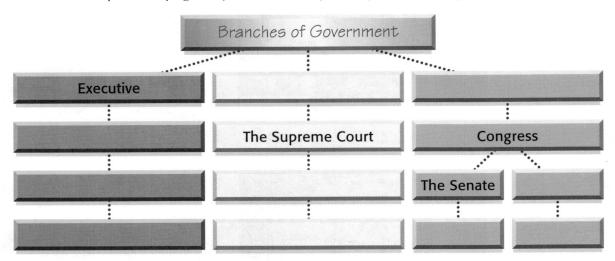

```
                    Branches of Government


  Executive                                          Congress

                    The Supreme Court

                                          The Senate
```

2. Look at the forms. Answer the questions.

Name: Hassan Al-Bahraini **Date of Birth:** 8/13/91	**Name:** Yoko Tanaka **Date of Birth:** 2/9/61
Address: 25 Colony St. **Lived there** 8 years	**Address:** 209 Gorham St. **Lived there** 4 years
Houston, TX 77036	Los Angeles, CA 90049
Hassan Al-Bahraini 6/1/01	Yoko Tanaka 6/1/01
Signature **Date**	**Signature** **Date**
Name: Ana Suarez **Date of Birth:** 5/6/76	**Name:** Chen Lu **Date of Birth:** 11/11/86
Address: 38 Opechee Dr. **Lived there** 10 years	**Address:** 47 Bleecker St. **Lived there** 3 years
Miami, FL 33133	New York, NY 10005
Ana Suarez 6/1/01	Chen Lu 6/1/01
Signature **Date**	**Signature** **Date**

Who…?

a. has lived in the U.S. for five or more years   Hassan and Ana

b. is 18 years old or older   _____

c. can take a U.S. citizenship test now   _____

3. What about you? Have you ever…? Check (✓) **Yes** or **No**.

	YES	NO	IF YES, WHEN?
taken a citizenship test	☐	☐	_____
voted	☐	☐	_____
registered with Selective Service	☐	☐	_____
served on a jury	☐	☐	_____

Challenge Look at **page 184** in this book. Complete the information.

1. Look in your dictionary. Put the words in the correct category.

LAND		WATER
rain forest		

2. Complete the chart. Use words from Exercise 1.

a. largest	island		Greenland (Denmark)	840,000 sq. miles
b. highest	_____		Everest (Asia)	29,078 feet
c. largest	_____		Sahara (N. Africa)	3,500,000 sq. miles
d. largest	_____		Arabia	1,250,000 sq. miles
e. largest	lake		Caspian Sea (Asia/Europe)	143,244 sq. miles
f. longest	_____		Nile (Africa)	4,160 miles
g. deepest	_____		Pacific	12,924 feet
h. largest	_____		Bengal (S. Asia)	839,000 sq. miles
i. highest	_____		Angel (Venezuela)	3,212 feet

3. What about you? Check (✓) the places you've been to.

☐ waterfall   ☐ desert   ☐ ocean   ☐ Other: _____

Challenge   Look at **pages 122 and 123** in your dictionary. Write the names of two islands, two oceans, two peninsulas, and two rivers. Do not use the ones from Exercise 2.

1. Look in your dictionary. Cross out the word that doesn't belong. Write the category.

a. <u>Operations</u>	addition	division	~~trigonometry~~	subtraction
b. _____	parallel	rectangle	circle	oval
c. _____	radius	angle	diameter	circumference
d. _____	geometry	algebra	calculus	multiplication
e. _____	square	cone	sphere	cylinder
f. _____	straight	perpendicular	pyramid	curved
g. _____	side	cube	diagonal	angle
h. _____	difference	quotient	algebra	product

2. Label the pictures. Use the words in the box.

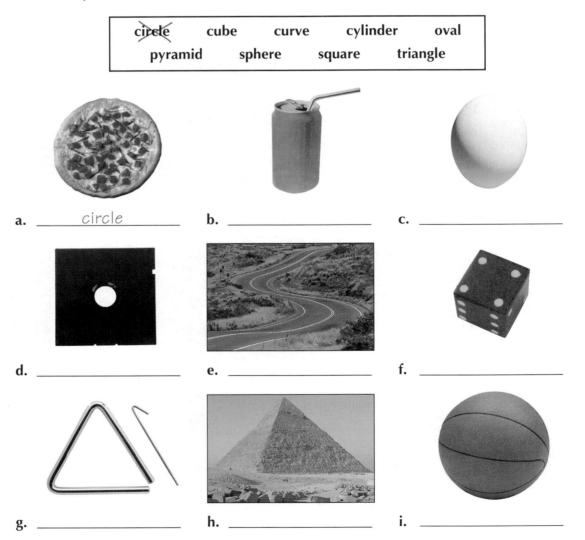

~~circle~~	cube	curve	cylinder	oval
pyramid	sphere	square	triangle	

a. _____circle_____   b. _____   c. _____

d. _____   e. _____   f. _____

g. _____   h. _____   i. _____

Challenge Look at Excercise 2. Think of more examples of lines, shapes, solids, parts of a circle, and parts of a square. Make a list.

1. Look in your dictionary. **True** or **False**?

  a. The <u>biology</u> teacher is observing something through a microscope. _____True_____

  b. The <u>physics</u> teacher is using a Bunsen burner. _____

  c. The <u>chemistry</u> teacher is writing a formula on the board. _____

  d. A molecule of water has <u>two</u> atoms. _____

2. Write the words in the box in alphabetical order on the lab inventory. Then look at the lab table. How many items are there? Complete the inventory.

crucible tongs	test tubes	funnels	~~beakers~~	graduated cylinders
	Bunsen burners	~~balances~~	petri dishes	slides
droppers	microscopes	magnets	dissection kits	forceps

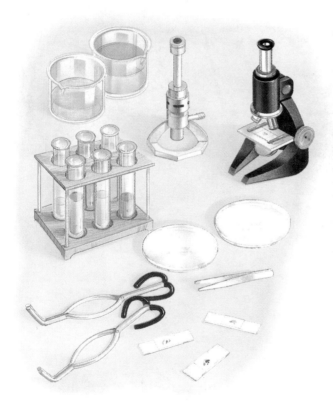

Lab Inventory

1. _____balances_____ 0
2. _____beakers_____ 2
3. _____ ____
4. _____ ____
5. _____ ____
6. _____ ____
7. _____ ____
8. _____ ____
9. _____ ____
10. _____ ____
11. _____ ____
12. _____ ____
13. _____ ____
14. _____ ____

3. What about you? Check (✔) the science classes you have taken. Circle the classes you would like to take.

  ☐ biology ☐ chemistry ☐ physics ☐ Other: _____

Challenge Change the <u>underlined</u> words in the false sentences in Exercise 1. Make the sentences true.

1. Look in your dictionary. Which instruments have…?

   a. strings   <u> violin </u>   <u>   </u>   <u>   </u>   <u>   </u>

   b. a keyboard   <u> piano </u>   <u>   </u>   <u>   </u>   <u>   </u>

2. Look at the bar graph. Number the instruments in order. (Number 1 = the instrument that the most people play)

Instruments People Play in the U.S.

Percent of Players (y-axis: 0, 5, 10, 15, 20, 25, 30, 35)

Based on 1997 Gallup Survey, reported in *Music USA,* 1997.

   <u>   </u> **a.** clarinet and drums

   <u>   </u> **b.** electric keyboard

   <u>   </u> **c.** flute

   <u>   </u> **d.** guitar

   <u>   </u> **e.** organ and violin

   <u> 1 </u> **f.** piano

   <u>   </u> **g.** saxophone and trumpet

3. What about you? Check (✓) the instruments you play. Circle the instruments you would like to learn.

   ☐ piano   ☐ clarinet   ☐ flute

   ☐ guitar   ☐ drums   ☐ electric keyboard

   ☐ cello   ☐ Other: <u>   </u>

Challenge   Find out about these instruments: viola, harmonica, harp, and bugle. What kinds of instruments are they? Look at the categories in your dictionary for help.

1. Look in your dictionary. In which class can you hear...?

a. **In 1996 the profit was higher.** _economics_

b. **This sphere is easy to draw.** _____

c. **Qu'est-ce que c'est?** _____

d. **It's cooking too fast.** _____

e. **What's the total?** _____

f. **Tra-la-la-la-la.** ♪♪♪ _____

g. **Turn left at that corner.** _____

h. **Only five more sit-ups!** _____

2. Look at the student's notes. Then complete the schedule with the words in the box.

TO DO THIS WEEK:
MON: Take test on road signs
TUES: Take test on irregular verbs (buy-make)
WED: Make bookshelf
THURS: Bring disk and software
FRI: Sing Mozart's Requiem (auditorium)

chorus	computer science
driver's education	
English as a second language	
shop	

Mon.	Tues.	Wed.	Thurs.	Fri.
driver's education				

3. What about you? Check (✓) the subjects you have taken. Circle the subjects you would like to take.

☐ art   ☐ business education   ☐ computer science
☐ economics   ☐ home economics   ☐ physical education
☐ shop   ☐ theater arts   ☐ Other: _____

Challenge Find out which of the subjects in Exercise 3 you can take at your school.

1. Look in your dictionary. Answer the questions.

   a. Which states in the United States are on the Gulf of Mexico?

     _____Texas_____   _____   _____   _____

     _____

   b. Which parts of Canada are on the Hudson Bay?

     _____   _____   _____   _____

   c. Which states in Mexico touch the United States?

     _____   _____   _____   _____

     _____

   d. Which countries in Central America are on the Pacific Ocean?

     _____   _____   _____   _____

     _____   _____

   e. Name four islands in the Caribbean Sea.

     _____   _____   _____   _____

2. Label the parts of Canada and the United States. You can use your dictionary for help.

In Canada:

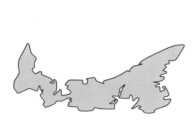  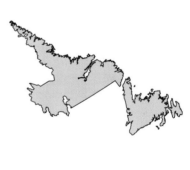

a. _Prince Edward Island_   **b.** _____   **c.** _____

In the United States:

d. _____   **e.** _____   **f.** _____

3. Look in your dictionary. Circle the words to complete the sentences.

In the United States:

a. California is north / (south) of Oregon.

b. Idaho is north / south of Utah.

c. Wisconsin is east / west of Minnesota.

In Canada:

d. Alberta is east / west of British Columbia.

e. The Yukon Territory is east / west of the Northwest Territories.

f. Nova Scotia is east / west of New Brunswick.

In Central America:

g. Nicaragua is north / south of Costa Rica.

h. Honduras is northeast / northwest of El Salvador.

i. Guatemala is southeast / southwest of Belize.

4. Match the state or province with the region and the country. Write a number and a letter for each item. You can use your dictionary for help.

STATE OR PROVINCE	REGION	COUNTRY
5, A **a.** Alberta	**1.** The Atlantic Provinces	**A.** Canada
_____ **b.** Campeche	**2.** The Midwest	**B.** Mexico
_____ **c.** Illinois	**3.** New England	**C.** The United States
_____ **d.** Massachusetts	**4.** The Pacific Northwest	
_____ **e.** Nova Scotia	**5.** The Prairie Provinces	
_____ **f.** Sonora	**6.** The Yucatan Peninsula	

5. What about you? Look at the map in your dictionary. Where have you visited? When were you there? Write sentences.

Example: *I drove to Nova Scotia in 1997.*

_____ _____

_____

_____

_____

_____

_____

Challenge Imagine you are driving from Manitoba, Canada to Durango, Mexico. List in order the states you will drive through.

1. Look in your dictionary. Cross out the country that doesn't belong.

a. North America	Canada	United States	~~Chile~~	Mexico
b. Asia	China	Poland	India	Philippines
c. Europe	Latvia	Ukraine	Belarus	Kazakhstan
d. Africa	Namibia	Peru	Botswana	Sudan
e. South America	Brazil	Paraguay	Guatemala	Colombia
f. Asia	Syria	Iran	Saudi Arabia	Romania
g. Europe	Greenland	France	Germany	Turkey

2. List the countries in the box in order of population size. (Number 1 = the most people) You can use your dictionary for help.

Argentina	**Belarus**	**Iraq**	**Italy**	**Kenya**	**Mexico**
	~~**Pakistan**~~		**South Korea**		

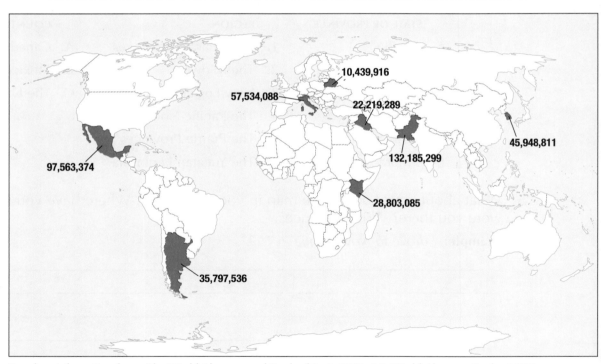

Based on information from: *The World Almanac and Book of Facts 1998.* (NJ: World Almanac Books, 1997)

1. <u> Pakistan </u> 3. _____ 5. _____ 7. _____

2. _____ 4. _____ 6. _____ 8. _____

3. Look in your dictionary. How many neighbors does ... have? Write the names of the countries.

a. In Europe:

Romania   <u>5</u>   <u>Moldova, Bulgaria, Ukraine, Serbia, Hungary</u>

b. In South America:

Paraguay   ___   _____

c. In Africa:

Chad   ___   _____

d. In Asia:

Thailand   ___   _____

e. In North America:

Mexico   ___   _____

4. Match the oceans with their size. Write the number.

<u>3</u>   **a.** Indian   **1.** 64,186,300 square miles

___   **b.** Atlantic   **2.** 33,420,000 square miles

___   **c.** Arctic   **3.** 28,350,500 square miles

___   **d.** Pacific   **4.** 5,105,700 square miles

Based on information from: *The World Almanac and Book of Facts 1998.* (NJ: World Almanac Books, 1997)

5. What about you? Complete the information.

MY COUNTRY	CONTINENT	NUMBER OF NEIGHBORS	POPULATION
_____	_____	_____	_____

Write the names of your country's neighbors.

_____

Challenge   Look at **page 185** in this book. Complete the information.

1. Look in your dictionary. Which forms of energy come from…?

ATOMS   THE EARTH   WATER

_____nuclear_____   _____   _____

                              _____

AIR   THE SUN

_____   _____   _____

2. Match the newspaper headlines with the types of pollution. Write the letter.

a. **BEACHES SAFE FOR SWIMMING THIS SUMMER**

b. Cars Get New Anti-Smog Device

c. *Farmers Stop Using Dangerous Chemicals On Grapes*

d. *Countries Agree To Stop Making Atomic Bombs*

e. **Petroco Cleans Up Water After Boating Accident**

f. *Report Shows Hospitals More Careful With Medical Garbage*

__f__ **1.** hazardous waste   ___ **3.** oil spill   ___ **5.** radiation

___ **2.** water pollution   ___ **4.** pesticide poisoning   ___ **6.** air pollution

3. What are the people doing? Use the words in the box.

recycling	~~saving energy~~	saving energy	saving water

a. I always turn off the lights.

_____saving energy_____

b. I turn the faucet off while I brush my teeth.

_____

c. I return cans and bottles to the store.

_____

d. I always use public transportation.

_____

4. What about you? Check (✓) the conservation steps you take. I….

☐ recycle   ☐ conserve water   ☐ conserve energy   ☐ Other: _____

Challenge Look at Exercise 3. List three other ways to conserve water or energy.

1. Look in your dictionary. **True** or **False**?

a. There are ten planets in our solar system. _____False_____

b. Saturn has rings. _____

c. The astronaut is looking through a telescope at the space station. _____

d. The astronomer is at an observatory. _____

e. There are six stars in the constellation. _____

2. Complete the chart with the names of the planets. Then answer the questions.

Which planet...?

a. is closest to the sun _____Mercury_____

b. is farthest from the sun _____

c. is the largest _____

d. has rings _____

e. is between Uranus and Pluto _____

f. is our home _____

3. What about you? What can you see in the night sky? Check (✓) **Yes** or **No**.

	YES	NO	
planets	☐	☐	If yes, which one(s)? _____
the moon	☐	☐	If yes, which phase? ☐ new ☐ full ☐ quarter ☐ crescent
stars	☐	☐	
constellations	☐	☐	
comets	☐	☐	

Challenge Find out the names of different constellations. What do they look like?

▶ **Go to page 178 for Another Look (Unit 9).**

Trees and Plants

1. Look in your dictionary. **True** or **False**?

   a. A tree has roots.   _True_

   b. Holly is a plant.   _____

   c. The birch tree has yellow leaves.   _____

   d. The magnolia and dogwood have pink flowers.   _____

   e. The cactus has a trunk.   _____

   f. Poison sumac has berries.   _____

   g. Poison ivy has needles.   _____

   h. The willow has cones.   _____

   i. The oak has branches and twigs.   _____

2. Look at the bar graph. Number the trees in order of height. (Number 1 = the tallest)

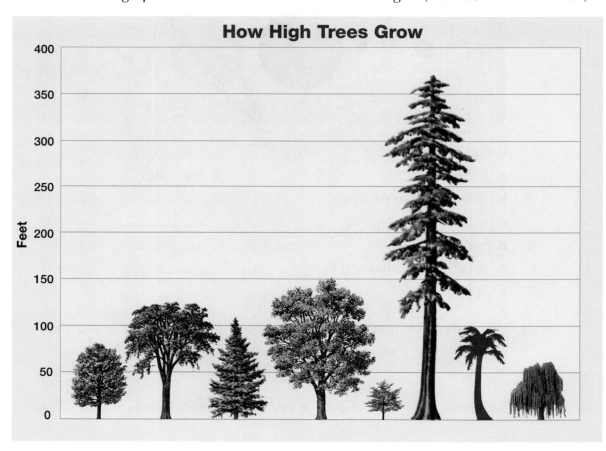

Based on information from: Petrides, G.: *Peterson Field Guides: Trees and Shrubs.* (NY: Houghton-Mifflin Co., 1986)

___ dogwood   ___ maple   ___ palm   _1_ redwood

___ elm   ___ oak   ___ pine   ___ willow

Challenge Which trees grow near your home? Make a list.

1. Look in your dictionary. What color is the…?

   a. tulip   _____pink_____   **e.** gardenia   _____

   b. daisy   _____   **f.** jasmine   _____

   c. crocus   _____   **g.** daffodil   _____

   d. poinsettia _____   **h.** carnation _____

2. Put the words in the box in the correct part of the diagram.

bud	bulb
leaf	petal
root	~~seed~~
stem	thorn

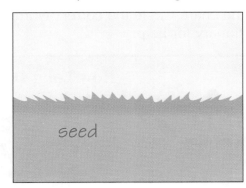

above the ground

seed

below the ground

3. Match the states with the flowers. Write the number. Look at **pages 122 and 123** in your dictionary for help.

Some U.S. State Flowers

   _3_ **a.** Kansas   **1.** iris

   ___ **b.** Illinois   **2.** rose

   ___ **c.** New York   **3.** sunflower

   ___ **d.** Tennessee   **4.** violet

   ___ **e.** Hawaii   **5.** hibiscus

4. What about you? Do you have flowers in your…? Check (✓) **Yes** or **No**.

	YES	NO	IF YES, WHAT KIND(S)?
home	☐	☐	_____
garden	☐	☐	_____

Challenge Find out the names of some other state flowers. Make a list.

Marine Life, Amphibians, and Reptiles

1. Look in your dictionary. Cross out the word that doesn't belong. Write the category.

   a. <u>Reptiles</u>   turtle   alligator   ~~seal~~   crocodile

   b. _____   fin   gills   scales   scallop

   c. _____   shark   frog   toad   newt

   d. _____   sea lion   dolphin   lizard   otter

   e. _____   tuna   whale   shark   eel

2. Look at the chart. Circle the correct words to complete the sentences. You can use your dictionary for help.

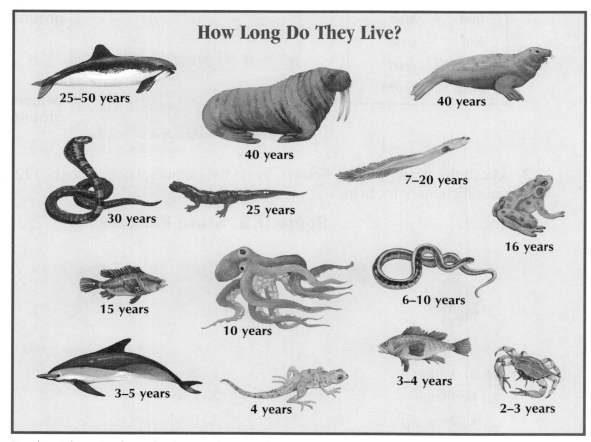

How Long Do They Live?

25–50 years

40 years

40 years

7–20 years

30 years

25 years

16 years

15 years

10 years

6–10 years

3–5 years

4 years

3–4 years

2–3 years

Based on information from: Shook, M. and R.: *It's About Time!* (NY: Penguin Books, 1992)

   a. The <u>frog / (octopus)</u> lives ten years.

   b. The <u>cod / bass</u> lives fifteen years.

   c. The <u>cobra / lizard</u> lives thirty years.

   d. The <u>porpoise / dolphin</u> only lives three to five years.

   e. The <u>eel / garter snake</u> can live to twenty years.

   f. The <u>crab / salamander</u> only lives a few years.

   g. The walrus and the <u>seal / dolphin</u> live forty years.

   h. The <u>cobra / garter snake</u> lives six to ten years.

3. Find and circle the 14 sea animal words. The words go → and ↓.

4. What about you? Make two lists using the words from Exercise 3.

THINGS I EAT:

_____

_____

_____

_____

_____

_____

THINGS I DON'T EAT:

_____

_____

_____

_____

_____

_____

Challenge Add to your lists in Exercise 4. Use your dictionary for help.

Birds, Insects, and Arachnids

1. Look in your dictionary. Complete the chart.

	NAME OF BIRD	HABITAT*	PHYSICAL APPEARANCE
a.	robin	■ ■ ▢ ■	Brown with orange breast.
b.		■ ■	Blue with white on wings, head, and breast.
c.		■ ■	Large. Brown with white head and tail. Big yellow beak and claws.
d.		■	Large head, flat face with big eyes. Brown and white feathers.
e.		■	Blue-black feathers with purple throat.
f.		■ ▢	Green with red throat. Long, thin bill.
g.		■	Large. Long black neck and head. White "chin" and breast.
h.		■	Black and white with small red spot on head. Small bill.
i.		■	Green head and neck. White neck "ring," brown chest and tail.
j.		■ ▢	Small. Brown, white and gray feathers.

*where the bird lives: ■ = forests   ■ = water   ■ = mountains   ▢ = farms   ▢ = suburban gardens   ■ = cities

2. Look at the picture. Check (✓) the insects in the garden.

☑ bee	☐ caterpillar	☐ grasshopper	☐ moth
☐ beetle	☐ cricket	☐ ladybug	☐ spider
☐ butterfly	☐ fly	☐ mosquito	☐ wasp

3. What about you? Make a list of the birds and insects you can see near your home.

Challenge Which insects "help" people? Which insects cause problems for people?

1. Look in your dictionary. Cross out the word that doesn't belong.

a. Pets	goldfish	guinea pig	~~squirrel~~	dog
b. Baby animals	sheep	puppy	kitten	baby chipmunk
c. Farm animals	horse	cow	gopher	pig
d. Rodents	rat	mouse	chipmunk	goat
e. Birds	parakeet	donkey	rooster	hen

2. Check (✓) the animals that are on the list of the Top Ten Pets in the United States.

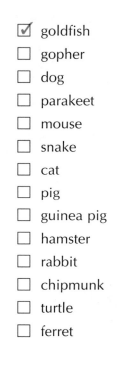

- ☑ goldfish
- ☐ gopher
- ☐ dog
- ☐ parakeet
- ☐ mouse
- ☐ snake
- ☐ cat
- ☐ pig
- ☐ guinea pig
- ☐ hamster
- ☐ rabbit
- ☐ chipmunk
- ☐ turtle
- ☐ ferret

Top Ten Pets

ferret

hamster

Based on information from: *The World Almanac for Kids 1997*. (NJ: World Almanac Books, 1996)

Challenge Survey your classmates. Find out if people have pets in their countries. Which ones are popular?

Mammals

1. Look in your dictionary. **True** or **False**?

   a. The beaver lives in North America.   _True_

   b. The lion lives in North America.   _____

   c. The koala lives in Africa.   _____

   d. The elephant lives in Asia.   _____

   e. The llama lives in South America.   _____

2. Look at the photographs. Circle the correct words to complete the statements.

   a. The antelope /(deer) has antlers / horns.
   b. The camel / llama has a hump / trunk.
   c. The bear / monkey has a long tail / neck.

   d. The elephant / rhinoceros has horns / tusks.
   e. The porcupine / platypus has long, sharp quills / whiskers.

   f. The lion / mountain lion has four hooves / paws.
   g. The kangaroo / hyena has a pouch / trunk.
   h. The skunk's / raccoon's coat /mane is black and white.

3. Look at these endangered* mammals.

United States

China and Italy

North America

Africa

Asia, Africa

Asia

China

Australia

Africa

South America

Asia

United States

Africa

Mongolia and China

Based on information from the Fish and Wildlife Service, U.S. Department of the Interior, as of 1998.

*endangered = very few still living; they may not continue to live

Check (✓) the animals that are endangered.

☐ moose	☐ gorilla	☐ coyote	☑ gray bat
☐ red wolf	☐ fox	☐ camel	☐ leopard
☐ armadillo	☐ mountain lion	☐ hippopotamus	☐ elephant
☐ anteater	☐ tiger	☐ opossum	☐ panther
☐ panda	☐ zebra	☐ koala	☐ black rhinoceros
☐ giraffe	☐ brown bear	☐ buffalo	☐ kangaroo

Challenge Write a paragraph about one of the animals in your dictionary. Where does it live? What does it eat? How long does it live? Is it endangered?

▶ Go to page 179 for Another Look (Unit 10).

1. Look in your dictionary. Who said...?

a. We caught a lot of salmon today!   *commercial fisher*

b. Do you want me to check the oil?   _____

c. These roses are for the people in apartment 5-G.   _____

d. This is the story of an elephant named Babar.   _____

e. Mmm. This soup smells good!   _____

f. You made $25,365.23 last year.   _____

g. Our plane lands at 2:20 P.M.   _____

2. Match the jobs with the tools. Write the number.

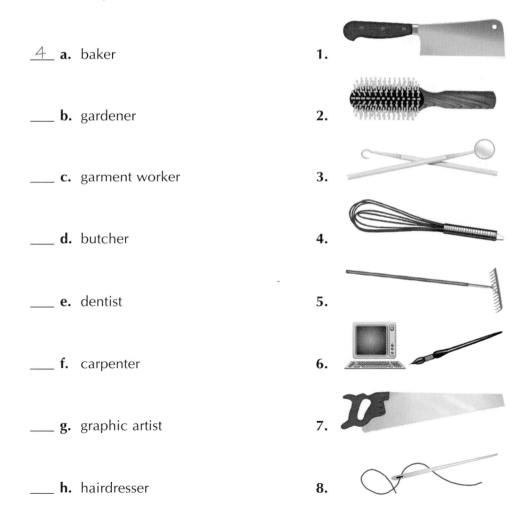

_4_ **a.** baker   **1.**

___ **b.** gardener   **2.**

___ **c.** garment worker   **3.**

___ **d.** butcher   **4.**

___ **e.** dentist   **5.**

___ **f.** carpenter   **6.**

___ **g.** graphic artist   **7.**

___ **h.** hairdresser   **8.**

3. Look in your dictionary. Put the jobs in the correct categories.

FOOD	CLOTHING	HEALTH	HOUSING
baker	_____	_____	_____
_____		_____	_____
_____		_____	_____
_____		_____	_____
_____			

4. Look at the bar graph.

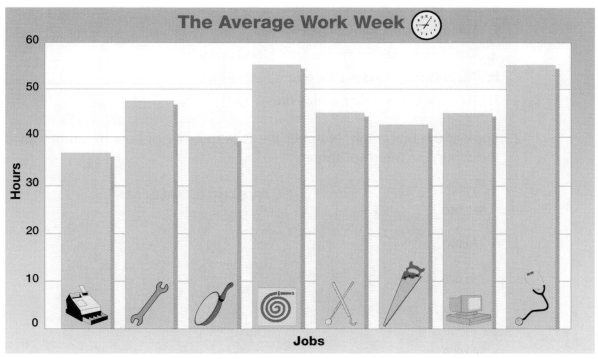

Based on information from: Krantz, L.: *Jobs Rated Almanac.* (NY: John Wiley & Sons Inc., 1995)

Who works…? Use the words in the box.

auto mechanic	carpenter	cashier	computer programmer
cook	dentist	doctor	firefighter

a. 37.5 hours a week _____cashier_____

b. 40 hours a week _____

c. 42.5 hours a week _____

d. 45 hours a week _____ and _____

e. 47.5 hours a week _____

f. 55 hours a week _____ and _____

Challenge Ask four people about their jobs. What do they do? How many hours a week do they work?
Example: *Meng is a cashier. She works 25 hours a week.*

137

1. Look in your dictionary. **True** or **False**? Put a question mark (**?**) if the information isn't there.

    a. The janitor is sweeping the floor.   _False_

    b. The interpreter can speak Spanish.   _____

    c. The printer is using a computer.   _____

    d. The machine operator is wearing safety glasses.   _____

    e. The lawyer is in court.   _____

    f. The movers are carrying a love seat.   _____

    g. The nurse is taking the patient's blood pressure.   _____

    h. The messenger rides a bicycle.   _____

    i. The model is wearing a blue dress.   _____

2. Look at the bar graph. Number the jobs in order of how much money people make. (Number 1 = the most money)

Based on information about U.S. salaries from: Krantz, L: *Jobs Rated Almanac.* (NY: John Wiley & Sons Inc., 1995)

    ____ **a.** travel agent   ____ **e.** machine operator

    ____ **b.** server   ____ **f.** painter

    ____ **c.** police officer   _1_ **g.** model

    ____ **d.** musician   ____ **h.** repair person

3. Look in your dictionary. Circle the correct words to complete the sentences.

   a. The housekeeper / (nurse) is wearing a white hat.

   b. The student / teacher is pointing to a map.

   c. The messenger / postal worker is holding packages.

   d. The receptionist / secretary is speaking to a man.

   e. The stock clerk's / store owner's name is Kim.

   f. The salesclerk / telemarketer is on the phone.

   g. The reporter / writer is on television.

   h. The serviceman / welder is wearing a mask.

4. Look at the job preference chart. Choose the right person for the job.

LIKES TO...	ARI	LUISA	TOM	CHRIS	MIA	DAVE
work with people			✓	✓	✓	
speak on the phone	✓					
be inside	✓	✓		✓		
be outside		✓			✓	✓
sell things	✓					
explain ideas				✓		
speak languages			✓			
travel			✓		✓	
repair things		✓				
help people			✓	✓		
wear a uniform					✓	
do physical work					✓	✓

   a. telemarketer _____Ari_____ **d.** welder _____

   b. instructor _____ **e.** mover _____

   c. serviceman/servicewoman _____ **f.** interpreter _____

5. What about you? Look at **pages 136–139** in your dictionary. Write the jobs.

   Jobs I can do now: _____

   Jobs I can't do now: _____

   Jobs I would like to do: _____

   Jobs I wouldn't like to do: _____

Challenge Look at your answers in Exercise 5. Explain your choices.

Job Skills

1. Look in your dictionary. Circle the job skills in the employment ads below. Write the name of the job. Use the words in the box.

Assembler	Caregiver	Chef	~~Manager~~	Orderly
	Salesperson	Secretary	Server	

a. ___Manager___
wanted to (supervise) staff at our small, friendly architectural company.
                              Call 555-2544.

b. _____
wanted to take care of small children. Must speak English and Spanish. Experience and references required.   555-3423

c. _____
wanted to assist medical patients at the new Riverside Nursing Home. Good income. Experience required.   Fax: 555-6545

d. _____
needed to assemble telephone parts in midtown factory. Immediate full-time employment.
                              Call 555-2134.

e. _____
needed to sell cars at our new Route 29 location. Must have experience and be able to work weekends.   555-0131

f. _____
needed for busy law office. Must work on a computer and type 50 words per minute. 9:00–5:00.
                              555-0034

g. _____
wanted to cook everything from hamburgers to duck l'orange at our small, neighborhood restaurant. The Corner Bistro, 230 Park Street.

h. _____
needed to wait on customers at a busy downtown coffee shop. Part-time only. Experience preferred.
                              555-1168

2. What about you? Check (✓) the job skills you have. Circle the skills you want to learn.

☐ drive a truck
☐ operate heavy machinery
☐ cook
☐ use a computer
☐ use a cash register

☐ supervise people
☐ speak another language
☐ repair appliances
☐ do manual labor
☐ Other: _____

Challenge   Choose two job ads from Exercise 1. Can you do the jobs? Why or why not?

1. Look in your dictionary. Fill out Dan King's job application.

EJ'S MARKET   **EMPLOYMENT APPLICATION**

Name: _Dan King_____   **Job applying for:** _____

1. How did you hear about this job? (Please check <u>all</u> appropriate boxes.)

☐ friends ☐ classifieds ☐ school counselor ☐ job board ☐ help wanted sign

2. Hours: ☐ part-time ☑ full-time

3. Have you had any experience? ☐ yes ☐ no **If yes, where?**_____

4. References _Sam Parker, Manager, Shopmark Supermarket_____

- - - - - - - - - - - - - - - - - - **For Office Use Only** - - - - - - - - - - - - - - - - - - -

Interviewed by: _Mr. Hill_____

Hired? ☐ yes ☐ no **Salary:**_____

2. Match the job applicant's words with what she is doing. Write the number.

_3_ **a.** (What's the starting pay?)   **1.** She's asking about benefits.

___ **b.** (Great. When can I start?)   **2.** She's talking about her experience.

___ **c.** (Hello. I saw your help-wanted ad. Is the job still available?)   **3.** She's inquiring about the salary.

___ **d.** (I worked at C.L. Thompson for two years.)   **4.** She's getting hired.

___ **e.** (What about vacation time?)   **5.** She's calling for information.

3. What about you? What do you think are the best ways to find a job? Number them in order. (Number 1 = the best)

___ look in the classifieds   ___ look for a help wanted sign   ___ talk to friends

___ look at a job board   ___ Other: _____

Challenge Survey your classmates. How did they find their jobs?

An Office

1. Look at the top picture in your dictionary. Where's the paper? Circle the office items that have paper in or on them.

(typewriter)   stapler   swivel chair   clipboard

desk pad   stacking tray   paper cutter   postal scale

calculator   supply cabinet   fax machine   paper shredder

2. Match the instructions with the office supplies. Write the number.

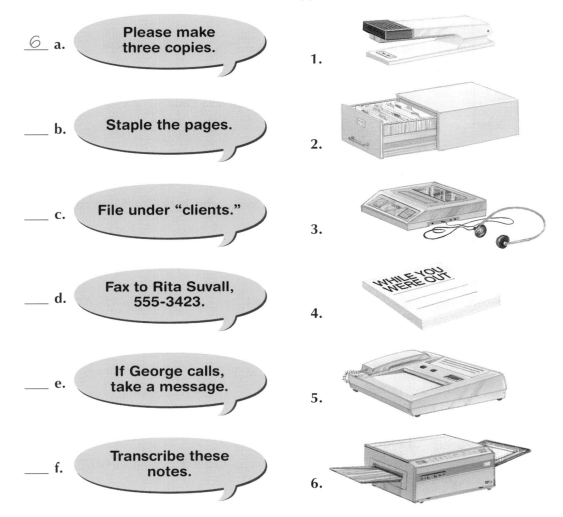

_6_ **a.** Please make three copies.

1.

___ **b.** Staple the pages.

2.

___ **c.** File under "clients."

3.

___ **d.** Fax to Rita Suvall, 555-3423.

4.

___ **e.** If George calls, take a message.

5.

___ **f.** Transcribe these notes.

6.

3. Look at the top picture in your dictionary. What can people use to find out...?

a. how many stamps a letter needs   _postal scale_

b. John Taylor's address   _____

c. the answer to 1,236 x 189   _____

d. today's date   _____

4. Look at the supply cabinet. Complete the office inventory. You can use your dictionary for help.

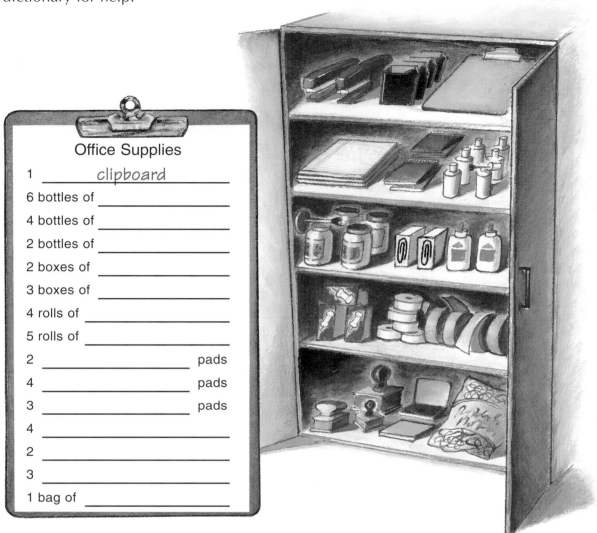

Office Supplies

1 _____clipboard_____

6 bottles of _____

4 bottles of _____

2 bottles of _____

2 boxes of _____

3 boxes of _____

4 rolls of _____

5 rolls of _____

2 _____ pads

4 _____ pads

3 _____ pads

4 _____

2 _____

3 _____

1 bag of _____

5. What about you? How often do you...? Check (✓) the correct columns.

	OFTEN	SOMETIMES	NEVER
type a letter			
use a fax machine			
collate papers			
file papers			
use Post-it notes			
use a pencil sharpener			
use an organizer			
use a desk calendar			
Other: _____			

Challenge Look at **page 185** in this book and answer the questions.

143

Computers

1. Look in your dictionary. <u>Underline</u> the dictionary words that are in the ad.

Multimedia Computer

FREE PRINTER WITH PURCHASE!

- 166mhz Pentium Processor
- 32MB SDRAM Memory
- 512KB Pipeline Burst Cache
- 3.2GB Hard Drive
- 17LS Monitor (15.7")
- 12X CD-ROM Drive
- Internal 335 Fax Modem
- 16-bit Stereo Sound Card
- Speakers
- 101-key Space Saver Keyboard
- MF Mouse
- Pre-loaded Software

$2399

2. Complete the ad. Use the words in the box.

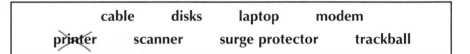

| cable | disks | laptop | modem |
| printer | scanner | surge protector | trackball |

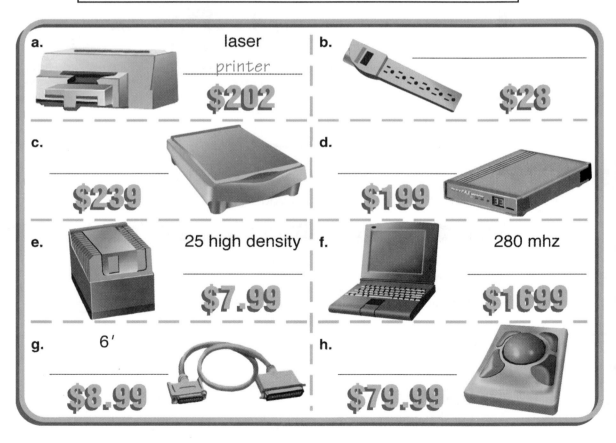

a. laser *printer* $202

b. _____ $28

c. _____ $239

d. _____ $199

e. 25 high density _____ $7.99

f. 280 mhz _____ $1699

g. 6' _____ $8.99

h. _____ $79.99

_____ **Challenge** Find a computer ad. <u>Underline</u> the words you know.

1. Look in your dictionary. Who said...?

a. Your dinner is here. ___room service___

b. I'm making the bed now. _____

c. That's $3.00, sir. _____

d. Please take the Smiths' luggage to room 365, Carl. _____

e. I'll put my clothes in the dresser. _____

f. You're in room 636, Ms. Jones. _____

2. Look at the guest room hotel directory. What number do you call for...?

Hotel Edison
a. room service   3
b. gift shop   —
c. pool   —
d. meeting room   —
e. front desk   —
f. housekeeper   —
g. bellhop   —

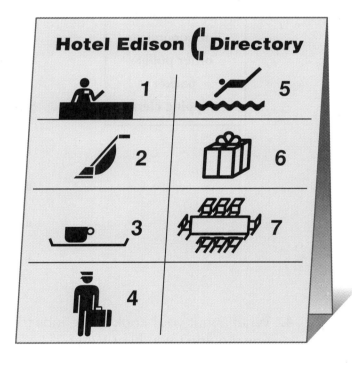

3. What about you? Would you like to be a guest at the hotel shown in your dictionary? Check (✓) **Yes** or **No**.

☐ Yes   ☐ No   Why? _____

_____**Challenge**   Look in your dictionary. Write five questions that you can ask the desk clerk about the hotel.
Example: *What time is the pool open?*

A Factory

1. Look in your dictionary. **True** or **False**?

   a. The factory manufactures lamps. _____True_____

   b. The factory owner is in the warehouse. _____

   c. The time clock is near the designer's office. _____

   d. The line supervisor and packer have clipboards. _____

   e. There are three boxes on the hand truck. _____

2. Cross out the word that doesn't belong.

a. **People**	designer	shipping clerk	~~forklift~~	packer
b. **Places**	time clock	warehouse	front office	loading dock
c. **Machines**	hand truck	order puller	forklift	conveyor belt
d. **Things workers do**	ship	design	manufacture	parts

3. Read the descriptions. Write the names of the jobs. Use the words in the box.

~~designer~~
factory worker
line supervisor
order puller
packer
shipping clerk

   ## Lamplighter, Inc.
   LAMPLIGHTER

   a. design the lamp _____designer_____

   b. watch the assembly line _____

   c. put together parts on the assembly line _____

   d. count boxes on the loading dock _____

   e. take boxes off the warehouse shelves _____

   f. put lamps in boxes on the conveyor belt _____

4. What about you? Look at the jobs in Exercise 3. Which one would you like? Which one wouldn't you like? Why?

   Example: *I would like to be a line supervisor. I like to supervise people.*

   _____

   _____

Challenge Rewrite the false sentences in Exercise 1. Make them true.

1. Look at **pages 136–139** in your dictionary. Who is wearing…?

a. a hard hat _____*engineer*_____ and _____

b. latex gloves _____ and _____

c. safety glasses _____

d. a back support _____

2. Label the safety symbols. Use the words in the box.

| biohazard   corrosive   electrical hazard   flammable   ~~poison~~   radioactive |

a. ____*poison*____   b. _____   c. _____

d. _____   e. _____   f. _____

3. Match the safety symbols in Exercise 2 with these situations. Write the letter.

__*f*__ **1.**   ___ **2.**   ___ **3.**

___ **4.**   ___ **5.**   ___ **6.**

4. Cross out the word that doesn't belong. Write the part of the body.

a. ____*ears*____   safety earmuffs   ~~respirator~~   earplugs

b. _____   hair net   back support   hard hat

c. _____   fire extinguisher   safety goggles   safety visor

d. _____   safety vest   toe guard   safety boot

5. What about you? Do you use any of the items in Exercise 4? Check (✔) **Yes** or **No**.

☐ Yes   ☐ No   If yes, which ones? _____

Challenge Which safety measures do you take at work? at home? Write a list for each.

Farming and Ranching

1. Look in your dictionary. Where can you find…? Write the locations.

    a. oranges   in the   <u> orchard </u>

    b. chickens   in front of the _____

    c. farmworkers   in the _____

    d. grapes   in the _____

    e. cattle   in and near the _____

    f. the rancher   on the _____

2. Look at the bar graph. Number the crops in order. (Number 1 = the biggest crop)

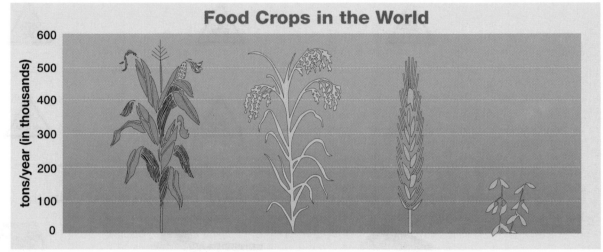

Based on information from: Ash, R.: *The Top Ten of Everything 1997*. (NY: DK Publishing Inc., 1996)

___ **a.** wheat   <u>1</u> **b.** corn   ___ **c.** rice   ___ **d.** soybeans

3. What about you? Have you ever been…? Check (✓) **Yes** or **No**.

	YES	NO	IF YES, WHERE?
a. in a field	☐	☐	_____
b. in an orchard	☐	☐	_____
c. on a tractor	☐	☐	_____
d. in a barn	☐	☐	_____
e. in a vineyard	☐	☐	_____
f. on a farm	☐	☐	_____
g. on a ranch	☐	☐	_____
h. in a corral	☐	☐	_____
i. in a vegetable garden	☐	☐	_____

_____ **Challenge** List products that come from wheat, soybeans, corn, cotton, and cattle.

1. Look in your dictionary. Put the words in the correct category.

HEAVY MACHINES	TOOLS	BUILDING MATERIAL
cherry picker	jackhammer	concrete
_____	_____	_____
_____	_____	_____
_____	_____	_____
	_____	_____
		_____
		_____
		_____
		_____

2. Match the jobs with the tools that the construction workers need. Write the number.

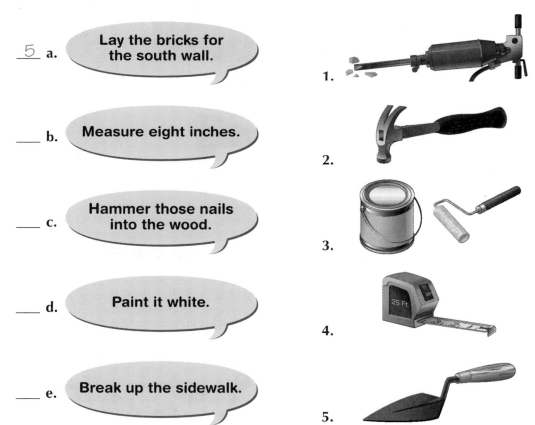

_5_ **a.** Lay the bricks for the south wall.

___ **b.** Measure eight inches.

___ **c.** Hammer those nails into the wood.

___ **d.** Paint it white.

___ **e.** Break up the sidewalk.

1.

2.

3.

4.

5.

Challenge Look in your dictionary. What are the construction workers doing? Write sentences.
Example: *One construction worker is using a jackhammer.*

Tools and Building Supplies

1. Look in your dictionary. Cross out the word that doesn't belong.

   a. Hardware   nail   bolt   ~~outlet~~   screw
   b. Plumbing   ax   plunger   pipe   fittings
   c. Power tools   circular saw   hammer   router   electric drill
   d. Paint   brush   roller   spray gun   chisel
   e. Electrical   wire stripper   drill bit   wire   extension cord
   f. Hand tools   hacksaw   flashlight   wrench   mallet

2. Look at the pictures. What do you need? Choose the correct tool from the box.

battery	drill bit	~~electrical tape~~	level
Phillips screwdriver	sandpaper	scraper	screwdriver

a. _electrical tape_   b. _____   c. _____

d. _____   e. _____   f. _____

g. _____   h. _____

3. Look at the picture. How many … are there?

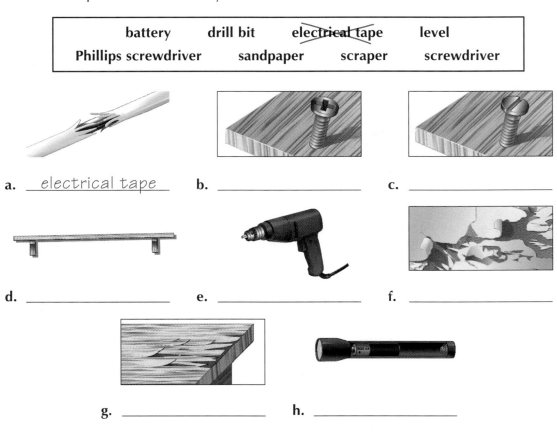

a. nuts _6_   **c.** screws ___   **e.** bolts ___
b. nails ___   **d.** washers ___   **f.** hooks ___

4. Look at the chart.

Pocket Tool Features							
Model							
Deluxe	●	●	●	●	●	●	●
Traditional	●	●	●		●	●	
Micro	●				●		●

True or **False**?

a. All three models have screwdrivers.   _____True_____

b. The "Micro" has a Phillips screwdriver.   _____

c. The "Traditional" has a saw blade.   _____

d. The "Micro" has a straight blade.   _____

e. All three models have a tape measure.   _____

f. Only the "Deluxe" has a wire stripper.   _____

g. The "Deluxe" has pliers.   _____

5. What about you? Check (✔) the tools you have.

- ☐ hammer
- ☐ handsaw
- ☐ power sander
- ☐ electric drill
- ☐ wrench
- ☐ mallet
- ☐ hacksaw
- ☐ screwdriver
- ☐ plunger
- ☐ level
- ☐ ax
- ☐ circular saw
- ☐ Phillips screwdriver
- ☐ plane
- ☐ chisel
- ☐ Other: _____

Challenge   Look at the chart in Exercise 4. Which model would you buy? What can you use it for?

▶ **Go to page 180 for Another Look (Unit 11).**

1. Look in your dictionary. Who said...?

a. I'm cutting the hedges.   *gardener*

b. And the score is: the Reds 6 and the Comets 4.   _____

c. I'm going to feed the elephants.   _____

2. Look in your dictionary. Circle all the dictionary words in the newspaper listing below.

What's Happening

Art
Newport (Art Museum) special exhibit of paintings by local artists. Through August 15. $4

Children
The Purple Players puppet show, Crown Amusement Park. Weekends, 2:00–3:00. Free.
Lincoln Square Annual Street Carnival. August 2–8, 10:00–8:00. Free.

Sports
Reds v. Kings baseball game, Hunter Field. August 11, 2:00. General admission: $2, Reserved seats: $4

General Interest
Union Square Flea Market, 10:00–6:00, every Sunday. Free.
Tiverton County Fair. Food, exhibitions, prizes. Admission: $5.50 adults, $3.00 kids.
Brosky Park Zoo, Elmwood Avenue. Special reptile exhibit until September 25. General admission: $5.00 adults, $2.50 children and senior citizens, free under 3.
Charles W. Smith Botanical Gardens. Flowers of every variety and color. Free.

At the Movies
Independence Day (***PG-13) Will Smith, Bill Pullman, Apple Valley: 12:45, 3:45, 7:00
Jack (**PG-13) Robin Williams, Fran Drescher, Castle: 12:45, 2:45

3. Where can you go to...? Use the circled words from Exercise 2.

a. see animals   *zoo*

b. watch pictures on a screen   _____

c. look at sculpture   _____

d. sit in a stadium   _____

e. buy merchandise at a booth   _____

f. go on small rides and play games   _____

g. see greenhouse flowers   _____

h. ride a big roller coaster   _____

4. What about you? Where would you like to go next weekend? Why?

_____

Challenge Look in a local newspaper or at the listing in Exercise 2. Talk to two classmates and agree on a place to go. Write your decision and give a reason.

1. Look in your dictionary. Where can you…?

    a. have a picnic   at the _____picnic table_____

    b. play baseball   on the _____

    c. ride a bicycle   on the _____

    d. get a drink   at the _____

2. Look at the park map. Complete the legend. Use the words in the box.

ball field	bike path	duck pond	picnic table
playground	~~tennis court~~	water fountain	

3. Look at the map in Exercise 2. **True** or **False**?

    a. There's a water fountain in the playground.   ____True____

    b. The tennis court is to the left of the ball field.   _____

    c. There's a seesaw in the playground.   _____

    d. There are benches near the duck pond.   _____

    e. The bike path goes around the duck pond.   _____

4. What about you? What did you do when you were a child? Check (✓) the boxes.

    ☐ ride a tricycle   ☐ picnic in the park   ☐ play on swings

    ☐ climb on the bars   ☐ play in the sandbox   ☐ go down the slide

    ☐ Other: _____

Challenge   Go to a neighborhood park or look at the park in your dictionary. What are the people doing? Write eight sentences. **Example:** *A little girl is riding a tricycle.*

Outdoor Recreation

1. Look in your dictionary. How many people are…?

a. hiking _2_ **d.** camping ___ **g.** rafting ___

b. mountain biking ___ **e.** fishing ___ **h.** backpacking ___

c. canoeing ___ **f.** horseback riding ___ **i.** boating ___

2. Read the situations. What do the people need? Use the words in the box.

camping stove	canteen	fishing pole	foam pad	insect repellent	~~lantern~~
	life vest	matches	multi-use knife	sleeping bag	

a. It's too dark. I can't read.   _lantern_

b. It's cold. Let's build a campfire.   _____

c. I'm thirsty.   _____

d. We need to cut this rope.   _____

e. Ouch! These mosquitoes keep biting me!   _____

f. Johnny is scared of the water.   _____

g. Everyone's hungry. I'll start the hamburgers.   _____

h. I'm tired. Good night.   _____

i. I can't sleep. The ground is too hard.   _____

j. I'd like to catch some of those trout in the lake.   _____

3. What about you? Which outdoor activities do you think are interesting? Number them in order. (Number 1 = the most interesting)

___ hiking   ___ mountain biking   ___ backpacking

___ rafting   ___ canoeing   ___ boating

___ fishing   ___ camping   ___ horseback riding

Challenge Look at Exercise 3. List the things you need for your number 1 activity.

1. Look in your dictionary. What are the people using to...?
   - a. build a sand castle ___sand___
   - b. sit on the sand __________ and __________
   - c. keep drinks and food cold __________
   - d. protect their skin from the sun __________ and __________
   - e. stay warm in the water __________
   - f. breathe under the water __________

2. Look at the chart. **True** or **False**?

Charles Beach	●		●			●	●
Moonstone Beach				●	●		●
Town Beach	●	●	●			●	

   - a. You can swim at Charles Beach. ___True___
   - b. You can use your surfboard only at Moonstone Beach. __________
   - c. You can go out in your sailboat at Town Beach. __________
   - d. You can use your scuba tank at Charles Beach. __________
   - e. You can rent a beach umbrella at Moonstone Beach. __________
   - f. There's a lifeguard at all three beaches. __________

3. What about you? How important are these things to you? Circle the number.

	VERY IMPORTANT			NOT IMPORTANT
clean sand	4	3	2	1	0
high waves	4	3	2	1	0
shade	4	3	2	1	0
seashells	4	3	2	1	0
lifeguard station	4	3	2	1	0
Other: __________	4	3	2	1	0

Challenge Look at the chart in Exercise 2. Which beach would you like? Why?

Sports Verbs

1. Look in your dictionary. Match the verbs with the sports. Write the number.

_5_ **a.** hit

___ **b.** swing

___ **c.** kick

___ **d.** shoot

___ **e.** ride

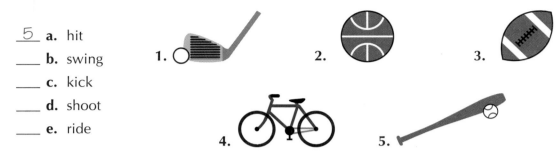

1. ◯

2.

3.

4.

5.

2. Look at the bar graph. Complete the sentences.

Based on information from Sutcliffe, A. (Editor): *Numbers: How Many, How Far, How Long, How Much.* (NY: HarperCollins, 1996)

a. When you _____jog_____, you burn 550 calories an hour.

b. When you _____, you burn 420 calories an hour.

c. When you _____, you burn 300 calories an hour.

d. When you _____, you burn 520 calories an hour.

e. When you _____, you burn 780 calories an hour.

f. When you _____, you burn 460 calories an hour.

g. When you _____, you burn 480 calories an hour.

3. Unscramble the sentences. Then look in your dictionary. **True** or **False**?

a. women in running Two are the park

_____Two women are running in the park._____ _____False_____

b. dribbling A is man the ball

_____ _____

c. is woman A stretching

_____ _____

d. into ocean diving A the is girl

_____ _____

e. A men tackling is man two

_____ _____

f. men are Three racing

_____ _____

g. man pitching is A a ball

_____ _____

4. Complete the analogies. Use the words in the box.

bend	finish	kick	pitch	serve	~~swim~~

a. ski : snow = _____swim_____ : water

b. throw : catch = start : _____

c. catch : hands = _____ : feet

d. shoot : basketball = _____ : baseball

e. shoot : arms = _____ : waist

f. swing : golf = _____ : tennis

5. What about you? Check (✔) the correct boxes.

HOW OFTEN DO YOU...?	OFTEN	SOMETIMES	NEVER	WHERE?
work out	☐	☐	☐	_____
dive	☐	☐	☐	_____
skate	☐	☐	☐	_____
ski	☐	☐	☐	_____
race	☐	☐	☐	_____
swim	☐	☐	☐	_____
Other: _____	☐	☐	☐	_____
_____	☐	☐	☐	_____

Challenge Rewrite the false sentences in Exercise 3. Make them true.

Team Sports

1. Look at the basketball court at the top of your dictionary page. Write the numbers.
   a. How many teams are there?   2
   b. How many fans are holding a sign?   _____
   c. How many players can you see?   _____
   d. How many coaches can you see?   _____
   e. How many referees are there?   _____
   f. What's the score?   _____

2. Write the name of the sport. Use the words in the box. You can use your dictionary for help.

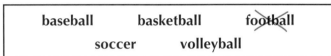

| baseball | basketball | ~~football~~ |
| soccer | volleyball | |

a. __football__   b. _____   c. _____

d. _____   e. _____

3. What about you? Circle the sports you have played. Underline the sports you have watched. Put a star (*) next to the sports you are a fan of.

   softball   football   basketball   baseball
   volleyball   ice hockey   water polo   soccer

_____ **Challenge** How many players are there on a … team? If you don't know, try to find out.

   basketball _____   baseball _____   football _____

   soccer _____   ice hockey _____   volleyball _____

1. Look in your dictionary. In which sports do you...?

HIT A BALL	RIDE	THROW SOMETHING
billiards		
	LIFT SOMETHING	USE A TARGET
STAND ON WHEELS	WEAR A MASK	WEAR A LEOTARD

2. Look at the chart. List the sports in order of popularity. (Number 1 = the most popular)

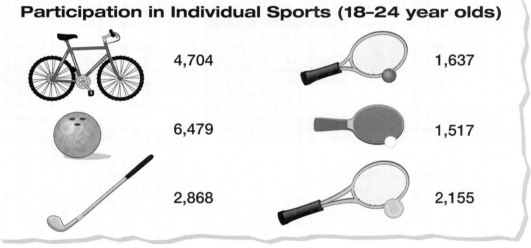

Participation in Individual Sports (18–24 year olds)

4,704		1,637	
6,479		1,517	
2,868		2,155	

Based on information from The National Sporting Goods Association, 1994. (based on survey of 10,000 homes)

1. __bowling__   4. _____

2. _____   5. _____

3. _____   6. _____

3. What about you? List three individual sports you participate in. (Number 1= the sport you do most often)

1. _____   2. _____   3. _____

___Challenge___ Interview at least four people. Which individual sports do they do? Make a list.
Example: *Two students do weightlifting.*

Winter Sports and Water Sports

1. Look in your dictionary. Circle the correct words to complete the sentences.

    a. The woman in the brown cap is (cross-country skiing) / downhill skiing.

    b. Two people are <u>snowboarding / sledding</u>.

    c. The man in black pants is <u>figure skating / ice skating</u>.

    d. A man and woman are <u>scuba diving / snorkeling</u>.

2. Look at the hotel information.

Where should these people stay? Write the hotel name(s).

    a. Ana likes water sports.   <u>Caribe Plaza or Mirror Lake Inn</u>

    b. Mei-Yuan likes winter sports.   _____

    c. Jason loves downhill skiing.   _____

    d. Crystal wants to go snorkeling.   _____

    e. Paulo wants to take his children sledding.   _____

    f. Kyle wants to go sailing and water-skiing.   _____

    g. Olga wants to go surfing.   _____

    h. Taro loves sailing and sailboarding.   _____

3. What about you? Look at the hotels in Exercise 2. Where would you like to stay? Why?

    Example: *I'd like to stay at the Wicker Inn or at the Hillside Lodge. I like skating.*

Challenge   Interview two people. Ask them which winter sports or water sports they like. Then recommend a hotel from Exercise 2.

1. Look in your dictionary. What do you see? Put the words in the box in the correct column.

arrow	~~bat~~	boots	bow	catcher's mask
club	glove	helmet	poles	racket
inline skates	shin guards	shoulder pads	target	uniform

BASEBALL	FOOTBALL	SKIING	ARCHERY
bat	_____	_____	_____
_____	_____	_____	_____
_____			_____

GOLF	TENNIS	SKATING	SOCCER
_____	_____	_____	_____

2. Look at the chart. Complete the list.

On an average day, Americans buy ...

3,014   6,153   8,493   6,619   33,973

Based on information from: Heymann, T.: *On an Average Day.* (NY: Ballantine Books, 1989)

a. 8,493   basketballs   **d.** 6,619   _____

b. 3,014   _____   **e.** 33,973 sets of   _____

c. 6,153   _____

3. What about you? Check (✓) the sports equipment you have used.

☐ bowling ball   ☐ football   ☐ ice skates   ☐ flying disc   ☐ baseball

☐ snowboard   ☐ skis   ☐ volleyball   ☐ weights   ☐ Other: _____

Challenge Look at **page 158** in your dictionary. Which sports equipment do you see? Make a list. You have only three minutes!

Hobbies and Games

1. Look in your dictionary. Cross out the word that doesn't belong.

a. Types of paint	~~clay~~	acrylic	oil	watercolor
b. Things to collect	baseball cards	clubs	stamps	coins
c. Cards	hearts	diamonds	spades	figurines
d. Games	cards	checkers	crochet	chess
e. Kits	doll making	woodworking	model	dice
f. Painting	brush	canvas	glue	easel

2. Look at the chart. Circle the words to complete the sentences.

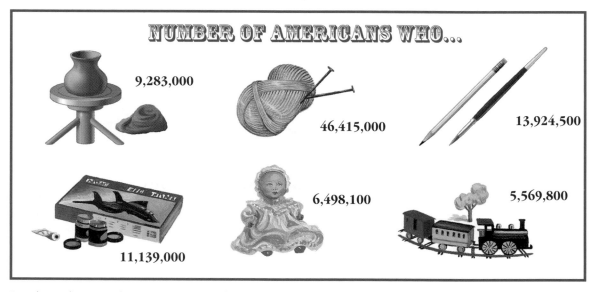

Based on information from: Heymann, T.: *The Unofficial U.S. Census.* (NY: Ballantine Books, 1991)

a. 46,415,000 people <u>collect things</u> / <u>(knit)</u> or do other needle crafts.

b. 6,498,100 people <u>collect dolls</u> / <u>make paper dolls</u>.

c. 13,924,500 people <u>paint</u> / <u>pretend</u> or draw.

d. 5,569,800 people have <u>action figures</u> / <u>model trains</u>.

e. 11,139,000 people <u>build models</u> / <u>play games</u>.

f. 9,283,000 people make things from <u>clay</u> / <u>yarn</u>.

3. What about you? Look at the hobbies in Exercise 2. Write them in the correct column.

HOBBIES I DO	HOBBIES I DON'T DO	HOBBIES I WOULD LIKE TO DO
_____	_____	_____
_____	_____	_____
_____	_____	_____
_____	_____	_____

4. Unscramble these hobby and game words. You can use your dictionary for help.

a. RODAB MAGE Ⓑ O A R D G A M Ⓔ

b. DIVOE MAGE _ _ ⃝ _ _ _ _ ⃝ _

c. RANY _ _ ⃝ _

d. GINFURIE _ _ _ _ _ ⃝ _ _

e. PREPA LOLD _ _ _ _ ⃝ _ ⃝ _ _

f. LACY _ _ _ ⃝

g. GRARTIDEC _ _ _ _ _ _ _ _ ⃝

Write the letters in the circles. Ⓑ ⃝ ⃝ ⃝ ⃝ ⃝ ⃝ ⃝ ⃝

Unscramble the letters in the circles.

A hobby: _ _ _ _ _ _ _ _ _

5. What is it? Use unscrambled words from Exercise 4 to write what the people are talking about.

a. I'm putting this dress on *her*.

paper doll

b. I'm going to make a bowl with *it*.

_____

c. Checkers is my favorite *one*.

_____

d. I'm using *it* to knit a sweater.

_____

6. What about you? How much do you like to...? Check (✓) the correct columns.

	I LOVE IT	I LIKE IT	IT'S OK	I DON'T LIKE IT	I DON'T KNOW
paint					
do crafts					
play cards					
collect things					
play board games					
Other: _____					

Challenge Look at **page 185** in this book. Complete the chart.

1. Look in your dictionary. Circle the correct words to complete the sentences.

   a. A (microphone) / remote control comes with the cassette recorder.

   b. The portable TV is to the left / right of the large television.

   c. The CD player is above / below the tuner.

   d. The clock radio is above / below the shortwave radio.

   e. The videocassette is inside / on the VCR.

   f. The young man is wearing earmuffs / headphones.

   g. The battery pack is to the left / right of the battery charger.

   h. The slide tray is on / next to the carousel slide projector.

   i. The video camera / 35 mm camera is to the left of the tripod.

2. Look at the ad. How much money can you save? Write the amount.

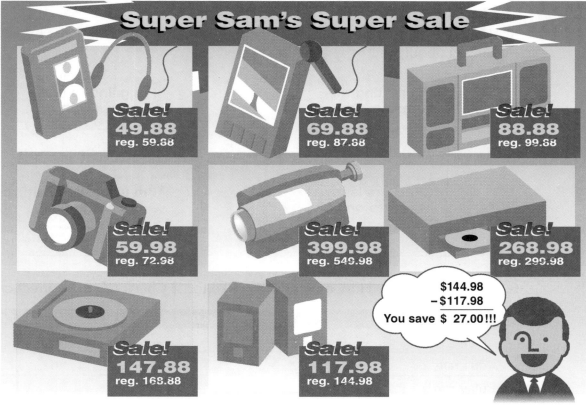

a. speakers	_$27.00_	**e.** portable radio-cassette player	_____
b. personal radio-cassette player	_____	**f.** cassette recorder	_____
c. CD player	_____	**g.** 35 mm camera	_____
d. camcorder	_____	**h.** turntable	_____

3. Look at the control buttons. Write the function. Use the words in the box.

| fast forward | pause | play | record | ~~rewind~~ | stop |

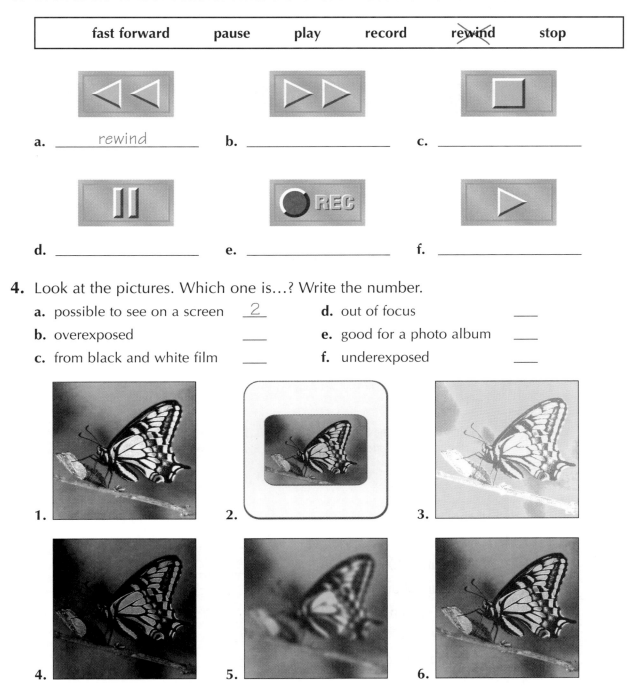

a. ___rewind___   **b.** _____   **c.** _____

d. _____   **e.** _____   **f.** _____

4. Look at the pictures. Which one is…? Write the number.

a. possible to see on a screen ___2___   **d.** out of focus ___

b. overexposed ___   **e.** good for a photo album ___

c. from black and white film ___   **f.** underexposed ___

1.   2.   3.

4.   5.   6.

5. What about you? Look at the ad in Exercise 2. Which item would you like to buy? Why?

_____

Challenge Find out today's prices for three of the items in Exercise 2. Compare the prices with the prices in the ad.

Entertainment

1. Look in your dictionary. Circle all the dictionary words in the TV schedule.

	8:00	8:30	9:00	9:30	10:00	10:30	11:00
	S A T U R D A Y			**E V E N I N G**			
2	**Entertainment Now** (Stand-up comedy) from L.A. clubs.	**Lisa!** Talk show host interviews soap opera stars.	**Movie:** Home Alone (1990 comedy). Family accidentally goes on vacation without 8-year-old son (Macaulay Culkin). Watch, but don't try it! ****				**News**
4	**Movie:** Mission Impossible (1996 action-adventure). Based on the popular television program. With Tom Cruise. ****				**Great Performances:** Bizet's opera Carmen. Performed live from Lincoln Center.		
5	**Wild World** Nature program looks at life in the jungle.	**Mystery!** Murder in a small town.			**The Twilight Zone** Visitors from Mars.		**News**
6	**Movie:** Marty (1955). Two lonely people find romance. Based on the play by Paddy Chayefsky.****		**How Things Work** A look inside the brain.		**Encore!** The New York City Ballet performs the Nutcracker Suite.		
7	**Time's Up!** New game show.	**The Simpsons** Cartoon.	**Movie:** Jaws (1975 horror). A large shark terrorizes tourists at a local beach. Directed by Steven Spielberg.*****				

2. Look at the TV schedule in Exercise 1. Write the time and channel if you want to....

    a. laugh at funny stories   _8:00, Channel 2_

    b. watch dancing   _____

    c. see a program about animals   _____

    d. watch a funny film   _____

    e. hear singing   _____

    f. watch a science fiction program   _____

    g. see a love story   _____

    h. learn what's happening in the world   _____ or _____

    i. be scared   _____ or _____

3. What about you? Look at the TV schedule in Exercise 1. What would you like to watch? Why? Try to use the words *serious, funny, sad, boring,* and *interesting.*

    Example: *I'd like to watch Science Watch. It sounds interesting.*

_____

4. Write the type of entertainment. Use the words in the box.

children's program	concert	~~quiz show~~	shopping program
science fiction story		soap opera	tragedy western

And the score is:
Alicia 25 and Todd 12.

a. _____quiz show_____

You can buy this
wonderful tool for only $29.99
plus shipping.

b. _____

Get off your horses, cowboys.

c. _____

Good-bye boys and girls.
See you tomorrow!

d. _____

Look! He's purple! And he has
three arms and two heads!

e. _____

I love you. I'll never
leave you. I want to marry you
and be with you. Always.

f. _____

Romeo and Juliet are dead!

g. _____

Next we will hear Beethoven's
Piano Sonata Number 3.

h. _____

5. What about you? What is your favorite TV program? Complete the information.

Name of program: _____

Type of program: _____

Day: _____

Time: _____

Channel: _____

Other information: _____

_____

_____

_____

Challenge Look at **page 185** in this book. Follow the instructions.

Holidays

1. Look in your dictionary. Write the holiday next to the date.

   a. July 4   <u>Independence Day</u>   d. Jan. 1   _____

   b. Feb. 14   _____   e. Dec. 25   _____

   c. Oct. 31   _____   f. 4th Thurs. in Nov.   _____

2. Write the names of the holidays on the cards. Then circle the correct words to complete the descriptions.

HAPPY
<u>New Year</u>   !

Happy
_____ !

   a. The card shows (confetti)/ fireworks.

   b. There's a <u>feast / jack-o'-lantern</u> on the card.

𝓗appy _____ !

𝓗appy
_____ !

   c. There's a <u>jack-o'-lantern / turkey</u>. It's part of a <u>costume / feast</u>.

   d. There's a red <u>heart / mask</u>.

Merry
_____ !

   e. There's a <u>flag / tree</u> with <u>confetti / ornaments</u>.

   _____ **Challenge** Make a holiday card.

A Party

1. Look in your dictionary. Who's...? Check (✓) the correct columns.

	TOM	SUE	THE GUESTS
a. planning a party	✓		
b. hiding			
c. blowing out candles			
d. answering the door			
e. decorating the house			
f. shouting "surprise!"			
g. lighting the candles			
h. singing "Happy Birthday"			
i. making a wish			
j. opening presents			

2. Melissa is planning a party. Look at her list and the picture. Cross out the things she has already done.

FOR THE PARTY
1. invite guests
2. buy gift
3. buy card
4. wrap gift
5. decorate house
6. bake cake
7. buy candles

3. What about you? Describe a party you went to.

Type of party: _____   Place: _____

Time: _____   Number of guests: _____

Check (✓) the things that happened. Did people...?

☐ decorate the room   ☐ shout "surprise!"   ☐ sing "Happy Birthday"

☐ light candles   ☐ open presents   ☐ Other: _____

Challenge Plan a party. Make a list of things you will do before the party and at the party.

▶ **Go to page 181 for Another Look (Unit 12).**

"C" Search

Look at the picture. There are more than 15 items that begin with the letter **c.**
Find and circle them.

Make a list of the items that you circled. Use your own paper.

Example: *coins*

Picture Crossword Puzzle

Complete the puzzle.

```
        ┌─┬─┬─┬─┬─┬─┬─┬─┬─┐
        │ │ │¹D│ │ │ │ │ │ │
        ├─┼─┼─┼─┼─┼─┼─┼─┼─┤
        │²│ │ I│ │ │ │ │ │³│
        ├─┼─┼─┼─┼─┼─┼─┼─┼─┤
        │ │ │ P│ │ │ │ │ │ │
        ├─┼─┼─┼─┼─┼⁴┼─┼─┼─┤
        │ │ │ L│ │ │ │ │ │ │
        ├─┼⁵┼─O┼─┼─┼─┼─┼─┼─┤
        │ │ │ M│ │⁶│ │ │⁷│
        ├⁸┼─┼─A┼⁹┼─┼─┼─┼─┤
        │ │ │ │ │ │ │ │ │
        ├──┼─┼─┼─┼─┼─┼─┼─┼─┤
        │¹⁰│ │ │ │ │ │ │ │ │
        └──┴─┴─┴─┴─┴─┴─┴─┴─┘
```

ACROSS

2.

8.

4.

10.

5.

DOWN

1.

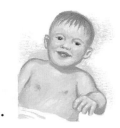

6.

2.

7.

3.

9.

Picture Word Search

Find and circle the 15 house words. The words go → and ↓.

```
H  U  G (M  A  I  L  B  O  X)
I  R  A  A  N  C  O  O  L  R
M  I  R  R  O  R  C  W  D  B
B  L  A  K  R  I  K  S  M  U
L  I  G  H  T  B  U  L  B  S
E  L  E  V  O  T  E  E  O  H
N  I  N  W  I  N  D  O  W  I
D  D  O  L  L  S  H  E  L  F
E  I  W  H  E  I  A  L  O  W
R  A  K  E  T  M  O  U  S  E
```

"C" Search

Look at the picture. There are more than 25 items that begin with the letter **c**. Find and circle them.

Make a list of the items that you circled. Use your own paper.

Example: *coconut*

Another Look (Unit 5)

Picture Word Search

Find and circle the 16 clothes words. The words go → and ↓.

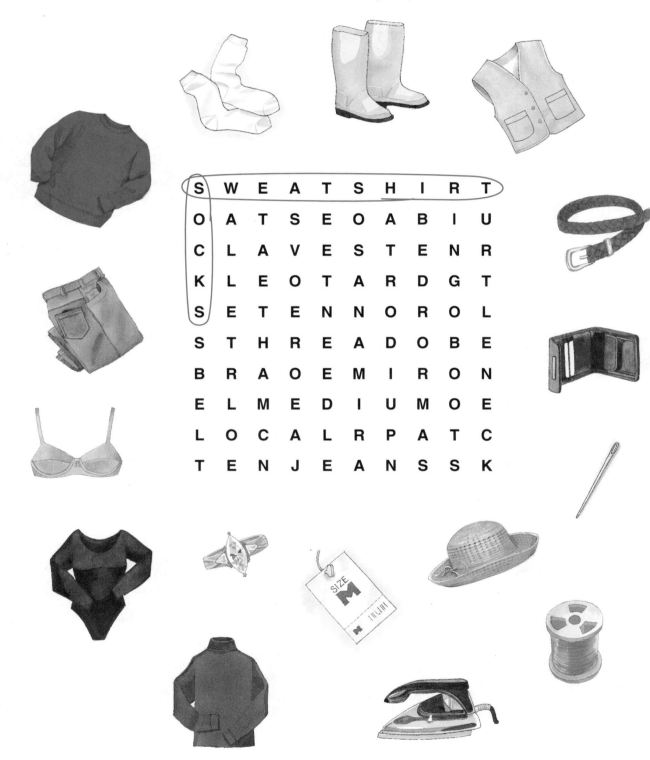

```
S  W  E  A  T  S  H  I  R  T
O  A  T  S  E  O  A  B  I  U
C  L  A  V  E  S  T  E  N  R
K  L  E  O  T  A  R  D  G  T
S  E  T  E  N  N  O  R  O  L
S  T  H  R  E  A  D  O  B  E
B  R  A  O  E  M  I  R  O  N
E  L  M  E  D  I  U  M  O  E
L  O  C  A  L  R  P  A  T  C
T  E  N  J  E  A  N  S  S  K
```

Picture Crossword Puzzle

Complete the puzzle.

¹T	A	²B	L	E	³T			⁴		
					⁵				⁶	
⁷										
⁸			⁹			¹⁰				
								¹¹		
		¹²		¹³						
¹⁴							¹⁵		¹⁶	
		¹⁷								

ACROSS

1.

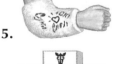
5.

7.

8.

11.

14.

15.

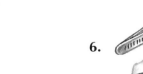
17.

DOWN

1.

2.

3.

4.

6.

9.

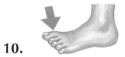
10.

12.

13.

15.

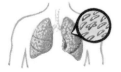
16.

"C" Search

Look at the picture. There are more than 12 items that begin with the letter **c**. Find and circle them.

Make a list of the items that you circled. Use your own paper.

Example: *coffee shop*

Where have all the flowers gone?

Look at the picture. Circle all the flowers.

Write the location of the flowers. Use your own paper.

Example: *on the bus*

Scrambled Notes

Unscramble the words for these areas of study.

English Composition
gEnshil poCmsooniti

rapagrhap _paragraph_

nestneec _____

locno _____

deti _____

thaM

aqsure _____

buce _____

midateer _____

lagerab _____

cisMu

lufet _____

onipa _____

putrmet _____

cacrodnio _____

greyohGap

aslind _____

eacon _____

verir _____

palsin _____

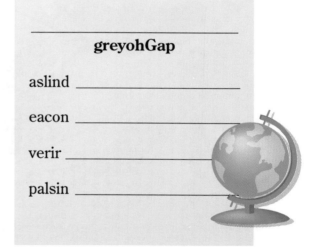

cicSeen

eldis _____

mota _____

msirp _____

mechisytr _____

heT vsUnieer

letecopse _____

rurMyec _____

lagyax _____

nocteslltanio _____

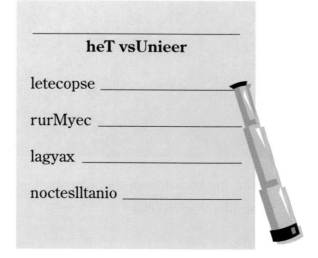

Picture Crossword Puzzle

Complete the puzzle.

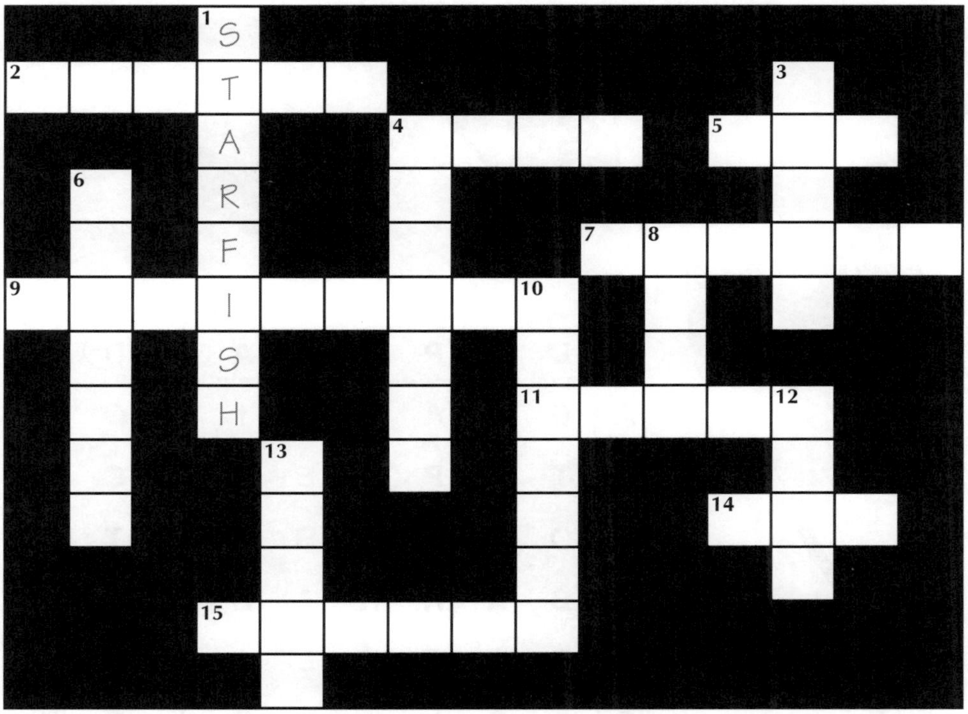

ACROSS

2. 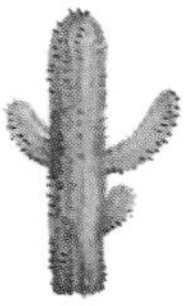

9. 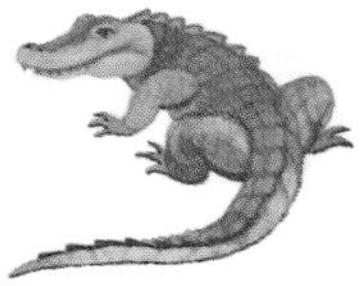

4. 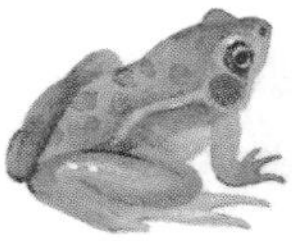

11. 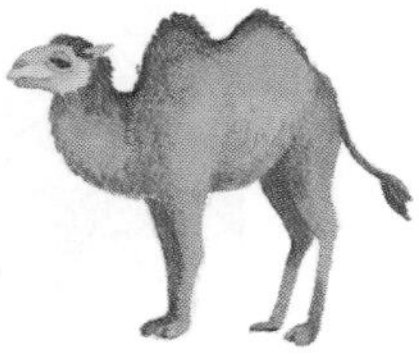

5. 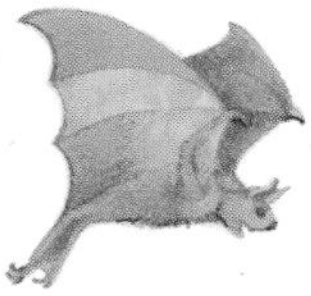

14. 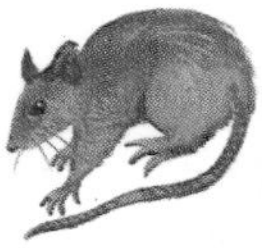

7. 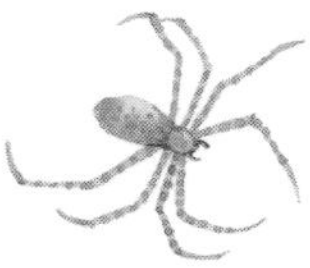

15. 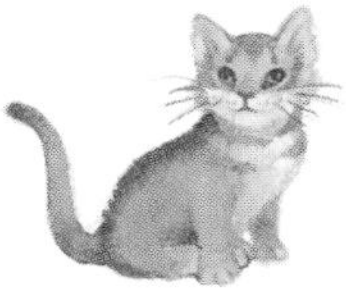

DOWN

1. 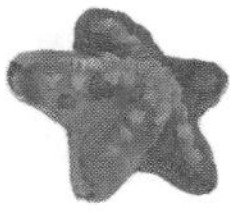

8. 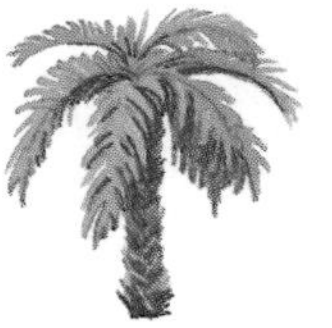

3. 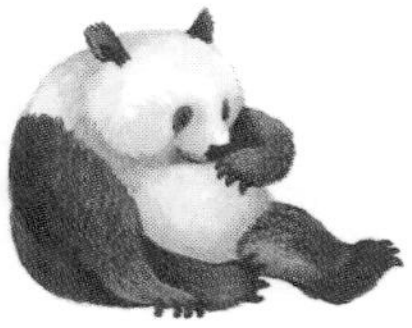

10. 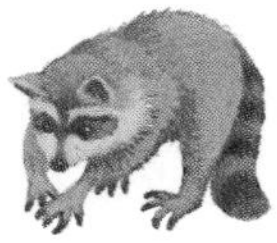

4. 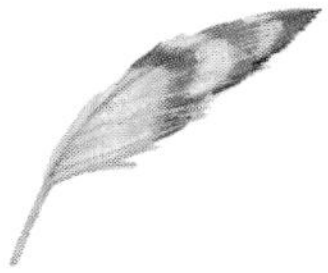

12. 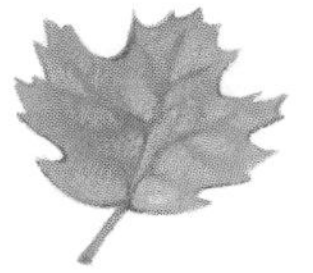

6. 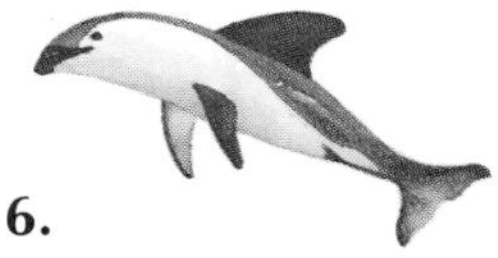

13. 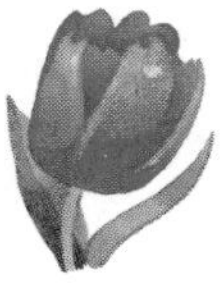

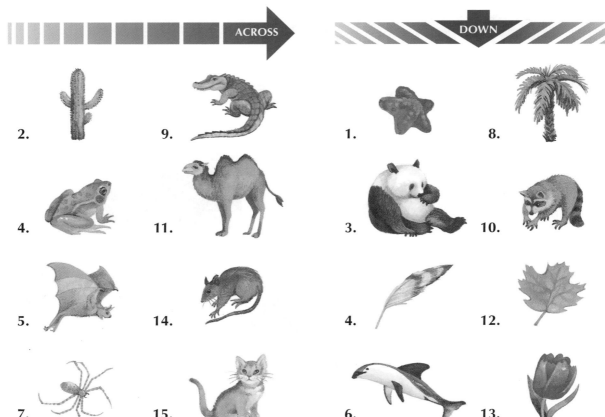

Picture Word Search

Find and circle the 16 work words. The words go → and ↓.

```
C  L  I  P  B  O  A  R  D  E
A  E  N  A  P  O  I  S  O  N
S  T  A  P  L  E  R  T  C  M
H  O  X  E  I  R  N  U  T  O
I  B  A  R  N  A  R  W  O  U
E  O  R  C  P  L  I  E  R  S
R  L  O  L  A  B  E  L  D  E
A  T  M  I  L  A  D  D  E  R
L  O  O  P  L  L  A  E  S  E
S  H  O  V  E  L  N  R  K  D
```

"C" Search

Look at the picture. There are more than 20 items and activities that begin with the letter *c*. Find and circle them.

Make a list of the items and activities that you circled. Use your own paper.

Example: *cooler*

Challenge for page 8

Lu is talking to her friend, Ana. Complete the conversation.

_____, Ana.

Hi!

Thanks!

Bye.

Lu greets Ana.   **Lu compliments Ana.**   **They end the conversation.**

Challenge for page 20

Which coins or bills do you need for a...?

a. _____

b. _____

c. _____

d. _____

e. _____

f. _____

Challenge for page 21

Complete the sales slip for the item.

```
Cheap Eddie's          6/11/02

   Every Day Is a Sale Day!

1 _____   _____
tax @ 6%              _____
Total                 _____
Amount tendered        $30.00
Change                _____

        Thank You
```

~~$30.00~~
$25.00

Challenge for pages 28–29

Complete the time line for yourself or someone you know.

Event

Year

Challenge for pages 30–31

What do you do when you feel…?

a. nervous   **b.** bored   **c.** homesick   **d.** confused   **e.** angry

Example: *When I feel nervous, I go for a walk.*

Challenge for page 57

Look at Exercise 2, a–d, on page 57 in this book. Change the U.S. measures to metric measures. Use the charts in your dictionary for help.

a. ____ 1¹/2 pounds ____ = ____ about 680.4 grams ____

b. _____ = _____

c. _____ = _____

d. _____ = _____

Challenge for page 85

Look at page 85 in this book. What does the doctor do? What does the dentist do? What do both the doctor and dentist do? Put the words from Exercise 2 in the correct space.

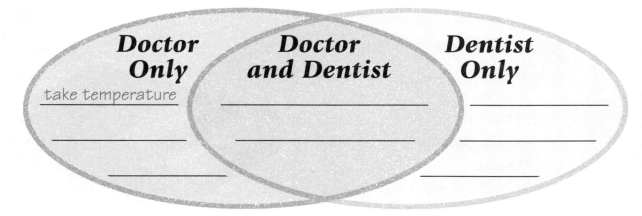

Doctor Only

take temperature

_____

_____

Doctor and Dentist

_____

_____

Dentist Only

_____

_____

Challenge for page 104

1. Survey your classmates. Which forms of transportation do they use? Complete the chart.

FORM OF TRANSPORTATION	NUMBER OF STUDENTS

2. Make a bar graph. Use the information from your chart in Exercise 1.

Challenge for page 116

Write the name(s) of…

a. the President of the U.S. _____

b. the Vice President of the U.S. _____

c. the Chief Justice _____

d. two U.S. Senators _____ and _____
(from your state, if you live in the U.S.)

e. one Congressman or Congresswoman _____
(from your state, if you live in the U.S.)

Challenge for pages 124–125

Complete the information for a classmate.

_____'S COUNTRY	CONTINENT	NUMBER OF NEIGHBORS	POPULATION

Write the names of the country's neighbors.

_____

Challenge for pages 142–143

What can you use these office supplies for? Which do you prefer? Why?

a. appointment book / desk calendar _____

b. typewriter / computer _____

c. telephone / fax _____

d. staples / paper clips _____

e. clear tape / packing tape _____

f. address book / rotary card file _____

g. file folders / big envelopes _____

Challenge for pages 162–163

Find out about some other games. Complete the chart.

NAME OF THE GAME	TYPE OF GAME (BOARD/CARD/VIDEO)	COUNTRY PEOPLE PLAY THE GAME IN	NUMBER OF PLAYERS

Challenge for pages 166–167

Look in the newspaper or ask classmates for the name of a....

sitcom _____

game show _____

sad movie _____

serious TV program _____

soap opera _____

radio program _____

talk show _____